letters to a
young chef

The Art of Mentoring from Basic Books

Letters to a Young Lawyer
Alan Dershowitz

Letters to a Young Contrarian
Christopher Hitchens

Letters to a Young Golfer
Bob Duval

Letters to a Young Conservative
Dinesh D'Souza

Letters to a Young Activist
Todd Gitlin

Letters to a Young Therapist
Mary Pipher

Letters to a Young Chef
Daniel Boulud

Letters to a Young Gymnast
Nadia Comaneci

Letters to a Young Catholic
George Weigel

Letters to a Young Actor
Robert Brustein

Letters to a Young Journalist
Samuel J. Freedman

Letters to a Young Mathematician
Ian Stewart

Also by Daniel Boulud

Café Boulud Cookbook:
French-American Recipes for the Home Cook

Cooking with Daniel Boulud

Daniel Boulud

letters to a
young chef

BASIC
BOOKS

A Member of the Perseus Books Group
New York

Hardcover first published in 2003 by Basic Books
Paperback published in 2006 by Basic Books
A Member of the Perseus Books Group

Books published by Basic Books are available at special discounts for
bulk purchases in the United States by corporations, institutions,
and other organizations. For more information, please contact the
Special Markets Department at the Perseus Books Group, 11 Cambridge Center, Cambridge MA 02142, or call (617) 252-5298, (800)
255-1514 or e-mail special.markets@perseusbooks.com.

Boulud, Daniel.
    Letters to a young chef / Daniel Boulud.
        p.   cm.
    Includes index.
    HC: ISBN-13 978-0-465-00735-6; ISBN 0-465-00735-X
    1. Boulud, Daniel—Biography. 2. Cookery. I. Title.
TX649.B56B68 2003
641.5'092—dc21   2003007426

    07 08 / 10 9 8 7 6 5 4 3

PBK: ISBN-13 978-0-465-00777-6; ISBN 0-465-00777-5

*To Alex Lee, whom I met as a passionate
young cook, and who worked alongside me as a
chef de cuisine from 1993 to 2003, for the thousands
of dishes we enjoyed cooking together.*

▊ Contents

DO YOU REALLY
WANT TO BE A CHEF?

Writing these letters to you has inevitably made me think of myself when I started out in this business more than thirty years ago. I had yet to see an avocado, taste a truffle or eat my first dollop of caviar, which happened to be a spoonful of beluga over a turbot braised in champagne sauce. You, on the other hand, having spent three years in cooking school, know a lot more about our craft than I did when I threw myself into this career when I was fourteen. I left our family farm in St. Pierre de Chandieu and went to work at Restaurant Nandron in Lyon.

I very soon got my first taste of truffle.

Chef Nandron had just shot a pheasant, grown autumn plump on overripe grapes and juniper berries: He marinated it in cognac and Madeira, stuffed it with foie gras and the first black truffles of the season then roasted it in juniper butter, with cabbage, salsify root and a chunk of country bacon. Even for a kid raised on the glorious food of the Rhône valley this was a sensual revelation. I knew how to hunt and cook a pheasant country style, but that was simple home cooking and this was real cuisine.

Restaurant Nandron was only ten miles down the road from home, but my little village remained much as it had been in the nineteenth century with the exception of cars and electricity. Lyon, on the other hand, was very much part of the modern world: huge, busy, full of cosmopolitan people with sophisticated tastes. It was a far cry from the Boulud farm, where finding a snake in the barn provided enough excitement for a week's worth of conversation. I loved restaurant work from the moment I tied on a crisp blue apron (only the chefs wore white). It didn't take me long to decide three things: I knew I loved to cook, I knew that I wanted to learn from the masters and I knew that being a chef was the only thing I wanted to be.

It was probably a stroke of luck that I did not know much more. In the beginning, I didn't have a clue how much it would take to go from a lowly worker in a French restaurant to creating a restaurant of my own in New York City; I now know that it takes much more than simply knowing how to cook.

People often make that mistake: they confuse skill in the kitchen with being a chef. I've had some wonderful people work for me who can cook damn well. They have the talent. They've learned from the best. And yet I know that they will fulfill their talents best by continuing to cook in a great restaurant rather than trying to run one as a chef or owner.

To be sure, you need to know all the basics: cooking, from savory to sweet, curing to baking, the almost mystical art of sauces, seasoning, spicing, texture and taste. Add to that an up-to-date knowledge or at least acquaintance with the evolving styles of the important contemporary chefs all over the world. Yet this is only the beginning. How to work with people, how to manage them in the cramped quarters and fiery heat of the kitchen, how to practice self-discipline and bring it out in others, where to find the best ingredients and how to squeeze every last penny out of them, how to move around the dining room and be genuinely interested in every customer, how to fulfill the constantly changing food fantasies of a demanding public—these are skills that have nothing to do with shaking the pan but everything to do with whether or not you have what it takes to be a successful chef.

This lengthy list is not meant to discourage you. What I really want is to lay out before you some things you need to consider now, as you begin your career. And as far as I'm concerned, being a chef of what I would call a gastronomic restaurant is a wonderful career. By this I mean a restaurant that in the spirit of the Michelin guide is "worth a journey," not just a detour. In these letters I will share with you lessons I have learned in the hope that they will help you figure out if this is really the life you want. Of one thing I am sure: The only way you are going to make the grade is if being a chef is indeed what you want most to be.

First, do not be in a hurry. Even if things fall into place perfectly, it will take you at least ten to fifteen years before you can truly call yourself a chef. You will need those years to acquire the culinary skills and absorb the management and people skills that you'll need as a chef.

So then the question becomes, How am I going to spend those beginning years? And I would answer that you should begin by spending at least two years traveling the world, working as you go, experiencing what is becoming an increasingly global cuisine. This is a luxury that I did not fully have in my early years. Once you have done that, spend a half dozen years working for the very best chefs you can find: Bear in mind, you will gain a lot more from making salad in the kitchen of a great restaurant then you will from attempting Lobster Thermidor in an average joint.

Sometimes you will be what we call a *stagiaire* (like an intern) and you may not even be paid. I know that sounds like being a medieval serf, but there's a lot of competition to get into the best kitchens and it may require that you do whatever it takes to get your foot in the door. Furthermore, once you have that kind of head start on your resume you will only advance by working harder and longer than the rest of the kitchen crew so that you become noticed by your chef. If you do this, you will have taken a tremendous first step, because that chef more than likely will give you a full-time position or provide a connection to a new job and more education in another restaurant with another talented chef.

I was very fortunate to begin my career in Lyon at a time when that part of France was at the forefront of a culinary revolution. I went from one great restaurant to another, learned as much as I could and was given more and more responsibility. I learned cooking. I observed a lot about what went into the front and back of the house. And I also learned something about luck.

In those years, when I worked in the kitchens of Roger Vergé, Michel Guérard and Georges Blanc—at three of the top restaurants in France—I never had the feeling that these chefs were merely lucky. They made their luck by working very hard, honing their skills and developing their art.

When you go to work in the kitchen of a great chef, chances are you'll learn as much or more from the sous-chefs around you and your fellow cooks in training. The best places attract the best people. You'll learn from them, compete with them, challenge them. Right now in my kitchens in New York, besides my mostly American cooks and chefs, we have people from China, Japan, Mexico, Brazil, Israel, Italy, Spain and France. Every one of them knows something about food in his or her country that none of the rest of us knows.

Sometimes this international polyglot makes me laugh at the mishmash of cultures in modern kitchens. We had one Japanese cook who was very good but handled everything—from a leaf of chervil to a lobster tail—with his chopsticks. He was fast and precise, so I learned that there is more than one way to do things right in the kitchen, but still the technique amused me because it looked so strange in a classique kitchen. With slicing, though, he had the greatest precision I have ever seen. He could slice radishes for our cucumber soup blindfolded and they would look like they had come out of an expensive mandolin.

So, with the advent of truly global cuisine, a chef's education is not as straight a path as the one I took when I went from my first job at Nandron in Lyon and two years later drove sixty miles up the road to Georges Blanc. For a young chef today, you can make part of the global tour that I mentioned earlier simply by working in the right kitchens in the wide range of cuisines available in most cosmopolitan areas.

After you spend five years or so going from kitchen to kitchen, it is time to put down some roots in one or two places and move up through the ranks. This is when you will take the steps that will make you a true chef. Although you may arrive with a beautiful résumé from some famous restaurants and think you are pretty hot stuff, take my word for it, you are not. Even if you are, it does not mean that much to your chef. He or she is interested only in what is needed in the kitchen.

Building your ego is not part of the game. This may be hard to swallow after having worked so hard for five years, but there is only room for one ego in a kitchen when the crush of service is on. Do not take it personally. Respect the chef and always give more than expected. Become a key part of the team. This truly will deepen your technique, knowledge and relationships. It is a critical chapter in your development as a chef. This is where you move from being someone who can cook very well to one who does it right every time—or almost every time. Your goal must be perfection.

For example, I was watching a guy make pizza the other day in Greenwich Village, spinning the dough, tossing it in the air, stretching it into a neat circle. I thought, "He's perfect. I love it. I wish I knew how to do that." Yet I also knew that to be in the same league I would have to spend at least a year at it. It is the same in a restaurant kitchen. You cannot be master of anything unless you work at it for a good long while and can really understand it.

I remember chefs at the restaurants where I apprenticed who had been doing the same thing for ten years and were perfect at it. For any number of reasons, this career path is no longer possible. Perhaps it is the point-and-click accelerated pace of our lives, the ambition to be famous right away or rapidly changing trends in food; whatever the reason, we all work in a charged atmosphere of speed, high expectations, high ambitions. No one can put in all the time that apprentices once did. You will feel tremendous pressure to move forward as your peers advance. To develop skills the old, slow way is not always practical, so I do not expect a young American chef to do that, but still we can expect perfection in some things and competence in others.

Take the example of an omelet. Here I expect perfection, and so would any chef you go to seeking a job. André Soltner, the legendary chef and owner of Lutèce, may never have looked at a résumé the way I might with a prospective young cook. Instead, he would say, "make me an omelet." He figured he could tell a lot simply from watching the way the applicant beat the eggs, handled the pan and tasted for seasoning.

I agree with Chef Soltner. When the young chef beats eggs, I observe if he uses a fork so that the eggs are aerated but not foamed. Then I look to see if he has a sure hand with seasoning. Next, does he mix little bits of cold butter into the egg mixture? Does the young chef pick any pan that comes to hand, or does he know that only one pan in a kitchen is used for omelets and that it will be a well-seasoned black steel pan? If the pan is dusty, does he wash it? I hope not. Washing removes the well-seasoned patina. Instead, the pan must be heated very hot and scoured with a handful of coarse salt. Then, rather than rinsing, does he dump the salt in the garbage and wipe the newly seasoned pan with clean paper? Of course, now that we have Teflon, the cleanup may be easier, but give me black steel every time.

Now the cooking. It should be a quick operation. Heat up the pan until the steel is very hot, hit it with some clarified butter or a touch of oil, then pour the eggs in the pan and stir fast enough that they do not curdle. Mix rapidly with the fork as you stir, moving the pan and fork in opposite circular motions until the eggs are cooked to a runny consistency. Then a crisp tap of the pan against the burner will even out the eggs into a smooth unwrinkled blanket. Seconds later, lift the handle of the pan and roll the omelet. Give a tap on the handle to flip the rolled omelet, then flip neatly onto the plate. The whole process takes mere minutes, comprises many steps, and in observing them you can instantly assess the level of skill and confidence of any candidate.

You may never be called upon to make an omelet in a fine dining restaurant, but you will need to strive for the same high level of precision in every aspect of your craft. Spending six months to a year at each station in a restaurant seems just about enough if you practice, keep improving and keep challenging yourself to make it perfect. The more you look at cooking, the more you realize it is always an unfinished education. There is truly no limit to how much you can learn.

Mine is not the only path you can take. Cooking schools produce thousands of graduates each year. They do not all end up apprenticing in my restaurant or a restaurant like it. Many go into hotels, clubs, cruise ships, resorts—all good careers. Those chefs must be very well organized, have good management skills and know how to control costs, all of which are skills that you also need in a gastronomic restaurant.

These are fine jobs but are often limited in creativity. Nothing sounds more boring to me than so-called

Continental food, which is the standard fare in hotels, cruise ships and banquet halls. From prime rib to lobster bisque, it is the same all over the world and has nothing to do with the region, the seasons, the new trends in cooking. I think what makes a restaurant interesting is the vision and personal style of the chef, not sameness everywhere. So, from my point of view, a career like that is limited, with a ceiling in terms of salary as well. You can reach that ceiling pretty quickly. I should add that with the fine dining revolution I expect that the level of food and compensation for the chef is bound to change as cruise ship passengers and hotel guests demand more to justify the relatively high expense of a cruise.

Or you may opt for working in someone else's restaurant. Being a cook is an honorable profession, even an art. There is the quiet satisfaction of doing a job well, but security, not money and renown, are its rewards. Still, it is a life.

If you are an entrepreneur, however, there is no limit to how far you can go or how much you can earn. It takes sacrifice. It will take an understanding that you will work very long hours and not have much of a personal life, but if it is your passion, as it is mine, you do not have much of a choice. You are going to have to do it so you might as well try to do it right.

Of course, there are only so many top restaurants that even great cities such as New York, San Francisco or Los Angeles can support. Does this mean that you have to make it there? Not anymore. You can be a chef in a smaller city, in such places as Cincinnati or Louisville or Madison, Wisconsin, or even in the countryside. Look at Patrick O'Connell at the Inn at Little Washington. I am certain that no one in Washington, D.C., in search of a gourmet meal ever drove to the petite town of Little Washington before Patrick built his restaurant. But O'Connell is a wonderful chef with a vision, and his restaurant has become a destination for gourmets all over the country. If you cook amazingly and create the right environment, the public will find a way to you. So that's why I tell today's very good sous-chefs in New York City who are feeling frustrated because they are not out on their own yet, "You could quickly become a superstar in a smaller city." America craves those kinds of restaurants, so the opportunities are there. The choice is yours.

■ MENTORS

You will not take the same path that I took, but nonetheless you will proceed from one job to the next as you develop your career. Where do you start? At this stage of the game, no doubt you have some friends who have gone on to good kitchens, or one of your teachers in culinary school noted your raw talent or maybe you have some family connections, but whatever the case, if you have been studying to be a chef for a few years, you probably know somebody somewhere. My advice is to try them first. It is a big world out there, but a small community of chefs; your goal in starting out is to get your foot in the door with a good one. Not one of the great ones necessarily, but someone who knows how to cook very well and, just as importantly, knows how to run a restaurant that maintains a reputation year in and year out. Be careful of the trendy place with the supermodel waitresses and so-so food. Look for a place where you can feel soul—in the food, in the people, in the room.

That first place you work in is an important step for you, because once you are connected within the chef family—especially at the level of restaurant you and I are both interested in—your second job will be a whole lot easier to find than the first. At some point you will be able to go to your chef and say you want to move on, and if you have done a good job and there is no room to advance in his kitchen, you can pretty much count on his picking up the phone and making a call for you. Nandron was only too happy to call Georges Blanc for me when that day came. Or maybe the sous-chef for whom you worked has moved on and you call him or maybe a friend of his sends out a call for help. Like most businesses, especially at the top, the restaurant business is one of connections, and you make connections quite obviously by meeting and working with the right people.

What I am talking about here is what people in every walk of life call building your résumé combined with serious networking. I have never hired anybody on the basis of a résumé alone. In fact, if that is all a person has to recommend him, something goes off in my head, and though perhaps not always fair, I wonder, "didn't he pay his dues at the last job?" Because if he or she had, someone is going to help that person get the next job.

So lesson number one: Always leave on a good note. If you sign on with somebody whom you look to as a mentor, it is important to make the commitment to stay for two years or so, largely because in the beginning, I promise, you will not be up to speed in the kitchen. By that I mean that your skills, knowledge and palate are still very much works-in-progress. Simply by taking you on, any chef is making an investment in you. You need to stay long enough to pay back that investment—so hopping from one place to the next is the surest way to burn bridges. And in the small world of good restaurants, you only need to burn one to damage your career. Doing the job well, always being prepared and accepting every task as a challenge are the best things you can do for your résumé. If you have to mail it in cold, save the stamp.

You may not know anybody at the top, but if you have any connection at all, use it. Now is the time to ask for an introduction to a good kitchen. Usually people are ready to take a chance on someone young and full of enthusiasm. You might not get paid very much for it. You might have to do a *stage* (internship). Many people have done one with me. The way I look at it, their compensation is learning from my organization. Also, while they are doing their *stage* they are simultaneously beginning to make those all-important contacts.

I can guarantee that you know more people in the business than I did when I started. I was barely a teenager when I went into the kitchen at Nandron. It was a very good restaurant in Lyon (two stars) but not the top, and I was at the bottom of the heap. I learned how to peel every vegetable, fillet every fish and pluck every game bird in the Lyon markets. I got my knife skills together. I learned the importance of *mise-en-place* (the term for the art of creating your recipe in "kit" form—that is, broken down into preproduced elements so that you are ready before the crush of service, at which point all you have to do is cook, finish and assemble it, rapidly).

As low man on the team, my job was to go to the market in Lyon first thing in the morning to pick up supplies. Guess who else was there? The obsessive and legendary chefs of Lyon and its environs who were in the vanguard of new French cooking: the Troisgros brothers, Paul Bocuse, Georges Blanc and Alain Chapel. For a chef, being in Lyon in those days was like being a musician in Liverpool when the Beatles were getting together. These were the guys who were changing the food world. They were at the market so early to make sure they got the very best ingredients before anybody else had a chance to buy them. There were beautiful vegetables from the farms of the Rhône and wild herbs and cheeses from the mountains of eastern France and glistening fish fresh from the Mediterranean and the Atlantic.

So even though I had the least desirable job in the restaurant, I also got to rub elbows with the greats. This does not mean that I was able or even tried to get a job with them; but I got to see how great chefs act and think and handle ingredients, and that was invaluable. Once the marketing was done, I would sit down at one of the local *bouchons* and have a bowl of tripe with them. They would open a bottle of Beaujolais (but I stuck with lemonade). The stories, the pungent rough language, the camaraderie made me feel on top of the world. Of course, they would rag me pretty hard in the way that old pros like to tease a young kid. But I ate it up. I was just so happy to be in their company.

After three years of apprenticeship with Nandron, I figured I had learned about all I was going to learn there. Nandron understood that and I was off to my next mentor. It was particularly right for me, because that chef, Georges Blanc, came as I did from a family that had a tradition of serving the so-called grandmother cuisine of the area. He was interested in refining this traditional food into haute cuisine. When I say we came from similar traditions, I also must point out that his family-style cuisine had become world famous at his mother's auberge, La Mère Blanc, a wonderful one-star restaurant along the old Wine Route down to Burgundy. But Blanc elevated that country food to an art. Something as simple as frog's legs, which you could get anywhere, he made so that his were the best frog's legs you could ever hope to have: perfectly crisp, perfectly salted, perfectly moist, perfectly balanced between the full aroma of garlic, shallots and the herbal accents of parsley and thyme.

As I look at the modern dining landscape and see first the advent of comfort food and then the reinvention of that food on modern American menus, I recognize a process that I first experienced working with Georges Blanc. So my strong advice to you, which I learned from a three-star Michelin chef, is "Remember your grandmother's food!" Grandmother is a short way of saying, remember the foods that connect you to your region, your family, your culture. For me, if I had to pick one dish that conjures up my background, it would be *Crêpes Vonnassienne*: mashed potato and crêpe batter made into crispy moist pancakes, soft with a buttery perfume. Or, if not that, then frog's legs or crayfish or *Poulet de Bresse* or wild hare or mallards from Le Dombes. See what I mean? It is like Proust and his madeleine: once you start thinking of one favorite dish from your childhood, it summons up a whole world. When you are a chef, you are going to want to honor your past by transforming food memories into offerings that belong in a great restaurant.

When you work with a great chef, your job is not to be creative but rather to interpret the creativity of the chef for whom you are working. The chef has an idea for a dish that comes from a deep understanding of cooking and ingredients. If you can help interpret his ideas, his inspiration and techniques, you will enrich your foundation as a chef.

For example, one day Georges Blanc had an idea for sorbet. It would be *Sorbet Cocktail aux Quatre Fruits*— sorbet cocktail with four fruits. He told us to use grapefruit juice, orange juice, a little bit of lemon, grenadine, banana, pineapple and some vanilla for balance. It was very important to him that you could taste and smell everything. He didn't want any one fruit to dominate so that the diner might think it was simple banana sorbet or just pineapple sorbet. It had to be an *everything* sorbet.

This recipe was all about balance. I was the one he asked to test and retest and measure and get it right. I can remember very vividly one afternoon when I made the *mise-en-place* for the recipe. I worked directly with Georges on this, and our one-on-one gave me a feeling of connection to him that one rarely had in the hustle and bustle of service. My responsibility was to make sure that I was creating the perfect sorbet. Blanc could approve it or if not, help guide me as to how to make it better. This was true whether the task was as simple as this sorbet or as inspired and complex as a *Poularde de Bresse* stuffed with crayfish, chicken liver, foie gras, porcini and truffle. During the experimentation phase of any dish, there is constant communication between the chef and cook, slowly bringing the dish into harmony with the chef's vision. Getting it right (which I did) was a tremendous satisfaction.

Blanc and Nandron were chefs in the Burgundian and Lyonnais tradition—founded on broad tastes as powerful as burgundy wine (which was used in many of the recipes). Blanc was an innovator, but his tastes always had an authentic link to the classically pungent flavors of the region. My next mentor was Roger Vergé at Le Moulin de Mougins on the French Riviera. In the same way that my job with Blanc resulted from a phone call from Nandron, another phone call, this time from Blanc, landed me with Vergé. The year was 1974.

The Burgundian Vergé had traveled the world and finally settled in the south, where he embraced the sunny, light cuisine of Provence—as bright as a Van Gogh sun-flower. His was probably the most fashionable and stylish restaurant in the world during the mid-1970s. It was a Mecca for the next generation of talented young chefs. Alain Ducasse was a chef there before he went on to become the most Michelin-starred chef ever. David Bouley, one of the most innovative and successful American chefs, also cooked there. These are guys who run world-class operations now. Yet they stayed on as sous-chefs at Vergé for a good long time, "banging on the ceiling" to rise to their natural position. Of course, that position at the top of the ladder was at a world-class restaurant, so they had to remain content banging on the best damn ceiling in the business while they learned from one of the top ten chefs in the world.

Those years served them, and me, well. It was my first three-star restaurant (Blanc was still a two when I was there) and a whole new level of the game. Working in such a stable of thoroughbreds made each of us better. We learned the same lesson that you will learn if you find a good restaurant with a good team: Although everything is based on the skill and reputation of the chef at the top, haute cuisine is a team sport.

In cooking another person's cuisine, discipline, not your creativity, is the most important quality. Expressing what the chef wants and doing so with his or her team requires it.

What did I learn with Vergé? Better to ask, What didn't I learn? Every one of my cooking skills was honed. I took the first baby steps as a manager, running the *garde-manger* (cold appetizers and soup) station and the braising station. I can still smell and taste his lamb shoulder that I made so many times. It was braised slowly overnight in a casserole sealed with bread dough so that not a waft of aroma or flavor escaped. It was rich in Provençal herbs fresh picked from Vergé's garden: rosemary, basil, thyme, bay leaf. To this he added a Middle Eastern accents with star anise, fennel, cinnamon and orange peel. Of course, the basic ingredients of a *Boeuf Bourguignon*—onions, carrots, mushrooms, turnips and celery—tied this dish to Vergé's Burgundian roots. The braising liquid was orange juice, red wine and olive oil (you heard me right, red wine and orange juice!). Fresh pork rind tied into small bundles gave body and a satiny unctuousness to the stew. What a novel, powerhouse idea! The result is a sublimely heady and fragrant stew—a marriage of simple ideas from many traditions that remained simple and yet unforgettable.

In addition to the deep braising of lamb, veal, beef and poultry, it was at the braising station where we did the initial prep for Vergé's sauces, which were the anchor of his cuisine. Sauces are their own discipline. Everything you know about flavor and balance is concentrated to the nth degree. What tastes too strong in the saucepan will mix spectacularly on the plate, and you have to be able to imagine the effect of the end result just by tasting what's in the pan. I remember a velvety sauce for duck made with the blood of the duck, giblets, a traditional *mirepoix*, Provençal herbs and figs. It was so complex yet so focused at the same time.

To this day, I merely have to hear the words *steak au poivre* to taste Vergé's reinvention of that traditional recipe with a *Sauce Mathurini*: cracked pepper, raisins, cognac, extremely full-flavored beef stock. Vergé could move easily from the big tastes of meat and game sauces to a whimsical *Sauce Poivre Rose*—a light creamy emulsion of paprika and sweet Sauternes, brought to a briny finish with Mediterranean rock lobster.

I learned cooking with all my mentors, but just as important, I observed the management side of cuisine, which is equally valuable to my success as a chef. As you move up through the ranks of a great kitchen, you pick up management by watching the people above you, watching the chef.

You may have all the creativity in the world, but it won't guarantee you success in a restaurant because if you cannot run a brigade of twenty people, you cannot run a restaurant. In order to learn to run that brigade of twenty, you must first learn to run a brigade of five or six—on the meat station, the fish station, the hot appetizer station: it does not matter which station, as long as you run it well.

Management is where the fantasy of being a chef runs into the business end. You go into cooking, no doubt, because you find it pleasurable. But business always comes before pleasure. The connection to your mentor, the understanding of what he or she does to run a successful business, these are things that you acquire over years.

Apparently I did, because after a few years, when I felt it was time to move on from Vergé, he had a surprise for me. "How would you like to go to Denmark and be sous-chef at a restaurant for me, teaching the Danish chef my cuisine?" he asked. "I think it will be a good test for you."

Hello? Denmark? That came out of left field. On the one hand, at twenty-one I still felt very young and inexperienced; yet I had absorbed a lot in my two years with Vergé. I had risen to *chef de partie* (meaning I managed a small group under the supervision of a sous-chef). This would be a big jump, though not exactly what I had planned. There were openings at another pair of three-star Michelin restaurants—Troisgros and Chapel—and I felt I had a pretty good shot at either place.

Denmark, though, was a whole new country (and I had seen very little of the world so far). It was really my first chance to indulge the chef's fantasy of taking his skills anywhere and making a living while learning a new culture. Our profession is one of the few that affords you this freedom. If you are a lawyer or a doctor or a stockbroker, you cannot just pull up stakes and start over in a new country or a bunch of new countries. As a chef, however, you take your knives and your passport and you chop onions in any country that will have you.

My year and a half in Denmark was a happy time. I rode my bicycle everywhere. I learned a lot about using such ingredients as caraway seed, cumin and other dried seeds that play such a large part in Nordic gastronomy (two words I had never put together before I went to Copenhagen). I learned independence away from the womb of French cooking. I picked up a good deal about managing people, but after a year and a half, I said, "I've done it. That's it. I've learned a lot, made better money than I have ever made but my education is not over." Again it was time to move on.

I heard from a friend whom I knew from Vergé, Didier Oudill, about an opening at Michel Guérard (see what I mean about friends and connections you make from one kitchen to the next?). I thought about it and decided, "Hey, I'm still young. I can afford to make (practically) no money and learn from the best." So I made the decision to go back to another three-star restaurant, slide back down the totem pole and take a big pay cut to do it. In the long run, though, I figured it would pay off.

Guérard, in Eugenie les Bains, was the high priest of lightness and ingredient-driven cuisine. He had taken an unusual route to chefdom—the pastry kitchen. Only after a successful pastry career in Paris did he embrace and advance the emerging style of nouvelle cuisine. Not only that, when he opened his first restaurant, Le Pot au Feu, it was in the blue-collar neighborhood of Asnieres. The food was so astonishing that soon this Bohemian bistro became the rage of Paris. Guérard learned from his mentor, Jean Delaveyne, an underrated but hugely influential chef who was among the forefathers of nouvelle cuisine.

So my new mentor had his own mentor. And you could trace Delaveyne no doubt back to Curnonsky, Gouffe and so on all the way back to the godfather of haute cuisine, Carême. It reminds me of the jazz legend Fats Waller playing organ and doing his own *stage* with an organist in Paris, who in turn had studied with a student of Franz Liszt. In any art, to connect with the great chain of masters stretching back through history is both humbling and exhilarating.

Guérard, partly by personality and by virtue of his background, created what I would call the haute couture of food—every detail done by hand and to measure. We made a rabbit casserole that included baby turnips (both the root and delicate greens), sage, savory, garlic sprouts and *ognoasse*, a purple onion found in the southwest. The vegetables and the rabbit cooked together, but in separate stages: their juices were constantly reduced, concentrated and combined. I compare this to haute couture—that is, preparation of each part of the recipe according to its requirements and perfectly married with equal care, because this is very much the way that a Parisian designer and his atelier bring together different elements of a dress.

At the same time, Guérard was almost spiritual about cooking and in that regard I have always thought of him as the poet of food. Precision in technique and poetry in approach—I cannot think of two better qualities for a chef. He taught me about perfection of the ingredient and the mission of the chef to present the true pristine flavors of each ingredient. Take his *Salade Gourmande* (in the 1980s, the fine dining world's most copied salad), for example: a green-bean salad, the haricots as thin as a needle, with shaved foie gras poached in duck fat (that is, confit), showered with slivers of black truffles, tossed with chervil and chive and crispy heart of lettuce. Very simple, but if it didn't have the perfect bean, cooked perfectly, the most delicate foie gras, the most pungent truffle, the most tender butter lettuce, the result would be pretentious and not very good. Every step had to be precise and perfect. Guérard was very patient, but he would not settle for less than your best. If you missed one step in a recipe that called for thirty-five ingredients, he would always know it—and you were dead meat.

With Guérard I arrived at a golden moment, in February, two months before his restaurant was to reopen for the season. Guérard had plans for a shop in Paris at Place de la Madeleine, right next to Hédiard and Fauchon, the world's greatest *épiceries*. So there were four of us—Guérard, Didier Oudill (chef de cuisine, or second in command), Jacky Lanusse (sous-chef) and me in this small town in France in the middle of nowhere. All we had to do was to create and test new dishes for the shop and restaurant.

Guérard was at his peak in his own zone—Planet Guérard. In this business, rarely does one get to work with such a great chef so closely and so directly in the act of creation. Sometimes when a chef writes a cookbook, a young chef collaborates on testing and refining dishes, so I was not the only one to have this experience, but with no restaurant pressures or book deadline, I felt a special grace.

Guérard's team would sometimes combine his vision with the techniques of kitchens we had worked in all over France. The result was a marriage of many master chefs through the intermingling of their "cooking genes" in the young chefs who had worked for them. So all that I said about subordinating your creativity to the vision of your chef in the end did result in our being called on to create in our own right.

This is the way of the world, not only in cooking. Work with a master. Learn to think like the master. And one day the master will have the confidence to ask you to move his work forward. When this happens, you are on your way to being your own master—or at least, you have taken a first step.

■ THE TRINITY OF HEAT

Becoming a chef, like making a good stock, needs unhurried, unpressured time. All cuisine starts with heating ingredients. Roasting, braising and sautéing are to my mind the key methods in the foundation of French cuisine. Other forms of heat have their uses—poaching, grilling, broiling, *sous vide* (low constant temperature with vacuum-sealed food), but in the classical kitchen the master of heat is first and foremost one who can roast, braise and sauté.

Cuisiner literally means to add heat to food. The idea is simple, the variations are infinite. Your range of temperatures is vast—from roughly 120°F for a slow confit of salmon in oil to 900°F for Tandoori lamb. When you understand heat, you "see" food down to its very molecules. You will sense that ingredients have been transformed by heat into something sensual and satisfying.

This mystical gift of sight and sensation is nothing more than the experience gained from making thousands of dishes so that a simple touch or smell will tell you exactly when something is done. Following a recipe by rote will never allow you to achieve this result. Every living thing is unique and will respond to heat differently. No two lambs, no two ducks, no two foie gras are exactly the same. Each must be watched, prodded and smelled until you sense, because you have cooked the recipe a thousand times before, that it is done. The recipe is at base nothing more than chemistry. The chef's job—to employ heat to transform ingredients—is the closest thing to alchemy I have come across. I know that this is nothing more than the result of years of work and practice; yet the results, when they are right, feel truly like the work of magic.

I once made a quail, for example, stuffed with foie gras and figs—three ingredients that require different cooking times. I could have roasted everything independently and made a nice dish, but I thought it would be more interesting all cooked together. If I stuffed the quail and roasted until the foie gras was done, I would have a bird the texture of denim stuffed with figs turned to runny mush and perfectly cooked foie gras. Clearly not my goal.

What I needed to do—*before* stuffing—was to presear and halfway cook the slice of foie gras and use ripe figs so that warming would just soften them. To execute this in the kitchen, logic required three steps in heating; understanding the interplay between heat and ingredients, however, allowed me to achieve a single combined recipe that produced a roasted whole quail split in half with perfectly pink breast meat, glistening foie gras and velvety soft fig.

A few years later, in preparing one of my quarterly fifteen-course blowouts for the renowned wine expert Bob Parker and his friends, I decided to up the ante and complicate the whole thing. I wanted to do a Ballotine (a boneless rolled and stuffed roast) of Duck, Foie Gras and Figs. I used a boneless butterflied duck stuffed with spiced ripe figs, wrapped in a thin slice of speck ham and whole foie gras marinated in Sauternes, salt, pepper and a spice mix of cinnamon, star anise, powdered clove and grated orange zest.

Once stuffed, the duck was trussed with twine. To finish, I had a range of different heat goals. This time I preroasted the foie gras (about one and a half pounds) in its own fat until it was half done. In other words, I didn't need the foie gras to be as precooked as in the quail, because by the time the duck was roasted to moist pinkness, it would allow the partially cooked foie gras time to release fat to infuse the figs, speck and duck meat. While the duck roasted, it was glazed and basted with spiced honey, salt and reduced citrus juice to give it a glistening crust. So I was striving to achieve different levels of doneness while controlling many ingredients, all with differing textures and flavors. Before serving, we presented it as Escoffier might have done: a silver platter that glittered like the full moon on the ocean, the glistening glazed ballotine in the center surrounded by a ring of endive caramelized in orange juice. Slicing the roast released a puff of sweet, spicy steam. On the plate you had a golden brown skin, an outer ring of rosy succulent duck, a firm and fatty foie gras and a sweet and salty boudin of fruit and ham. A spectacular dish—that Bob Parker still talks about. It is the challenge of creating new dishes like this that excites a chef.

See what I mean about so much to learn and the need for the time to learn it? So, let's get our aprons dirty and feel the heat of the line—the smoke, the steam, the sizzle of the noise of the chef's home (usually for more hours than his or her real home) . . . the kitchen.

The fundamental method of transforming food through heat is, to my mind, roasting. If the hearth is the heart of the home, the *rôtisserie* station is the heart of the restaurant. Roasting is not a fast process. When you roast, you cannot walk away from it the way you can leave a stock or a braised dish. You must stay connected to the food when you roast. You need to touch, smell and baste every so often. You need to add vegetables and garnishes at certain times so that they are finished just when the roast is finished. This keeps you on your toes.

At home, a great roast—say, a chicken—becomes the centerpiece of the day, both in the cooking and eating. The first consideration is the chicken. You need a good organic chicken—definitely not a plastic-wrapped factory farm chicken. Rinse it well, pat dry, then let it air dry in the fridge overnight so that the skin is no longer wet. Seasoning both inside and out is important. Add garlic, shallots, parsley and thyme in the cavity. Put two pats of butter on top of the chicken and place the chicken in a pan that is generously larger than the bird, but not so big that you could make a turkey in it. Place the pan in a 425° oven for half the cooking time (which depends on the size of the chicken, of course), basting with first-quality butter all the while. Halfway through the cooking I throw in a pound of small German butterball potatoes, a pound of cippolini onions and a whole head of garlic peeled and separated into cloves. Then a small bundle of fresh thyme and parsley stems and half-inch cubes of bacon or pancetta. Ten minutes later, add a pound of porcini or other meaty mushrooms. I lower the heat to 375° and let the chicken finish to golden brown juiciness. When the chicken is done, let it rest for twenty minutes and finish cooking the vegetables if they need it. Finally, toss in the parsley leaves. By the way, I call this Bill Blass Chicken, because Bill along with John Fairchild from *W* magazine used to order it frequently when I was the chef at the old Le Cirque.

In the restaurant, the *rôtisseur* might repeat this process for twenty chickens in a day, yet he or she must give the same care and attention to a half dozen things at once—from duck to chicken to squab to venison. Each has a different cycle of preparation. So, on the one hand, the *rôtisseur* must have an intuitive connection to each meat, and on the other, military precision.

It takes a very good cook to be a *rôtisseur*. As I mentioned before, all cooks want to work on the line—they think they are going to earn more respect if they are flipping pans. But roasting teaches you an understanding of main ingredients (meat, fowl, fish) that is deeper and that will make you a better chef on the line.

A good *rôtisseur* has only the outside of the meat to look at, but he or she must be able to imagine—very vividly—the transformation of juice, the firming of the flesh and the concentration of flavor that is going on deep inside. And then one must be able to think from there to the plate.

At the same time, you have to deal with the question of seasoning, an essential element in transforming merely hot meat into a precious moment of savory, succulent gastronomy.

Each cut of each animal has its own demands. Often you season before you roast, so that as the outer layer of meat caramelizes in the gentle searing of the initial exposure to heat, it pulls and concentrates flavor to the surface while gently penetrating the flesh. You may also season during the roasting. If it is a whole fowl or fish, then you season the cavity as well so that the seasoning permeates the flesh from the inside. At the completion of the process, the finished roast should be salted again so that as the meat relaxes and the juice reenters the flesh, it carries seasoning along with it. Finally, after slicing the meat, you lightly season again so that the first thing your taste buds react to is seasoning, opening up your palate.

Resting is nearly as important as roasting. You cannot rush roasting nor can you be in a rush to serve the roast. Meat must rest after roasting to maintain juiciness, and it is a cardinal rule of cuisine that holding the juices in the meat is the hallmark of properly roasted and served meat. How long? It depends on the meat. A thick cut of beef might rest half an hour or more, allowing the juices to be reabsorbed into the flesh (although the delicious, juicy, churrascaria style, is sliced fresh from the fire). Venison, a different story, is not very fatty—it does not have space in its fibers to absorb and hold moisture. If you leave it too long, the juices will leave the meat and you will be left with a bland, uninteresting taste. So, for example, my chestnut-crusted loin of venison is served very pink, because overcooked venison is unsalvageably tough and dry. I rest it for just a few minutes then slice it so that the juice and blood pearls on top of the slice. Then some sea salt and pepper, and it is perfect.

Next in importance to roasting is braising. Quite literally, *braising* means to cook on a *braisier*—that is, over red embers. Practically speaking, it involves cooking food that is barely immersed in liquid and slowly drawing out the fat and juice from meats as well as the juices and flavors from herbs and vegetables. It is all about slow cooking and basting, constantly basting. The braising pot is the cook's magic cauldron where flavors swirl, combine, concentrate, transform.

Braising, a rustic form of cooking widely used in every cuisine, is not without art nor the demand of the chef's constant attention. One thing it is not is simply putting some liquid and some meat in a pot, covering it and letting it bubble away for a few hours. Braising is not stewing. It is sort of half stewing and half-wet roasting. That is why basting is so important. As the flavors in the braising liquid concentrate, you keep basting and you build up a glacé on the meat that is both concentrated and flavorful. At the same time, you are reducing liquid: not only the liquid that you start braising with, but also the juices extracted by heating from the vegetables and meat. The reducing and glazing return these flavors to the meat.

If you end up with a lot of braising liquid, you have not concentrated the flavors enough. A properly braised piece of meat or fowl or fish has just enough liquid for that serving and no more. Do not shortchange your recipe. Give back to the plate every iota of flavor that the ingredients started with.

To me, braising is the deep soul of French cooking. Any dish that I think of with braising takes me on a culinary tour of France; for example, a lamb shank. If I think of Provence, I think of braising the lamb in garlic, herbs, orange zest, olives, tomatoes and a floral white wine. For the same piece of lamb in Burgundy, I taste a braising liquid of red wine, roasted onions, celery root, lard de campagne, wild mushrooms. Lamb shank in the southwest is going to braise with a more Spanish and mountain feel—lots of onions, peppers with some heat to them, tomatoes. At the other corner of France, it will be Alsatian *Baekenofe* style—lamb shoulder braised with pork shoulder, Riesling, onions and potatoes.

Braising reveals the beauty and depth—both historical and cultural—of French cooking. Not only does gastronomic cooking embrace all of these regions, refining their traditions, but it also draws on bistro cooking and cuisine bourgeoise (for purposes of illustration, the normal Sunday meal for a French family). In all French cuisine, braising is a major element.

Okay, I know you want to get to the line, so let's do it. The main activity on the meat and fish lines is sautéing. The textbook definition of sautéing is to cook something in a little bit of fat or oil and high heat. But in this simple definition there is a whole range of variations.

First the tools. I am not a big fan of aluminum—you can never get it really hot and things tend to stick to it (although it's fine for boiling or gentle roasting). Copper, though, can get very hot. When we make a chicken *jus* in a copper roasting pan, we heat the pan until it is super hot before we put the bones in to roast, which lets us begin with a quick sear and caramelization. Cast iron is also a great heat carrier: like copper, it gets very hot and distributes heat evenly. It is very good for caramelizing bones and meat before you deglaze. A word about meat caramelizing: You want it *brown*, not a light tan. The surface of well-caramelized meat develops sugars and nuttiness and a crust that not only seals in juice but creates a flavor and texture element that is delicious in its own right.

In the modern kitchen we use induction stoves that employ magnetic resonance; cast iron works very well with this high-tech method. For pan roasting, I like a black steel pan well seasoned with salt and oil, rinsed but never washed (just like the Chinese do with their woks). Stainless steel pans are easy to maintain but in practice, because things tend to stick in them, I prefer other materials.

With vegetables I like to let the flavor develop slowly and concentrate before I caramelize the outside. Many chefs blanch their vegetables then throw them into a hot pan with oil or butter. I feel that one preserves pristine flavor more fully when you put the vegetables in a pan, add a little bit of butter, sweet onion and a stem of rosemary, and slowly heat them, rolling them over and over in the butter (adding a few drops of water as needed). At this medium-low heat, they will be slightly steamed in their own moisture: *sweating* is a term we often use for this. With carrots, I start with a little butter (or olive oil) and chicken stock and fresh sage, then simmer until they are firm but getting tender. By this time, they have reabsorbed all their juices and released their sugars, which then glaze up beautifully. Covering the pan (for the initial wet cooking) with a lid or parchment aids this process enormously, allowing evaporation but at a rate that is, say, 20 percent, as opposed to 100 percent for an uncovered pan.

We also *arroser*: that is to say, baste with butter. Here, for example, a fish fillet is cooked in a hot pan. You keep spooning butter over the fish so that while it cooks and crisps on the bottom, hot butter seeps in and slowly

cooks the flesh on top. I think fresh cod responds beautifully to the sensual waves of flavorful heat that butter
carries, but almost any firm-fleshed fish is well suited to
this method.

In so much of what we have touched on in this letter—
whether it is extracting and reabsorbing juice in roasting,
or braising and reducing, or sautéing then caramelizing—
you are working the moisture in the food you are preparing; and then concentrating it, reintegrating it back into
the ingredient. Heat, concentrate, reintegrate. No matter
how you apply heat, this is the transformational aspect of
cuisine. How good your food is depends on how well you
control this force of nature.

■ YOUR SENSE
OF TASTE

Taste, the interplay of ingredients and textures, is very personal. Developing your sense of taste obviously is one of the most important aspects in becoming a chef. True, there are people who have fantastic palates who are not chefs. There are no chefs, however—or at least none of any note—who do not have a highly developed sense of taste. That sense will vary from chef to chef. One may express undercurrents of brininess, another may accent the herbal style of a region of mountain grasses and wildflowers, another, the hot and spicy kick that the end-less variety of chilies give to tamer ingredients. These accents, part personal and part cultural, make for the di-versity and delightful surprises in restaurant cuisine.

Taste is always present but not always perceptible. Analogously, when you listen to a symphony, you may hear the trumpets ring out, but you probably will not be able to distinguish between the violas and cellos, for example. Nonetheless, they are there and they are important. Remove one or the other and you may not be able to tell what exactly is missing, but you will know that the sound is somehow unbalanced, less than full.

It is the same with taste. In some recipes there is a dominating overall taste that may mask or at least mute the underlying levels of taste. In a pâté of Guinea Hen and Smoked Pork Belly, for example, the pleasantly gamey taste of cured and smoky pork will rise over the hen, foie gras and spices. Only after you bite and chew and breathe through your nose does the palate "round out" and let some of the subtastes come through: a delicious mélange of liver, mushroom, chestnut, sweet onion and garlic, the clarity of allspice and clove, the novel fragrance of pink peppercorn. All of these are nearly as important as the delicate piece of fowl that supports everything.

One thing that influences taste but which has nothing to do with taste buds is texture. With many dishes, your mouth seeks out texture first before it "decides" to experience taste. That is one of the fascinating things about taste: you prepare yourself mentally beforehand. Texture is a critical messenger in letting your taste know what is coming. The satiny smoothness then brittleness of chocolate, the chewy, sinewy unctuousness of a well-marbled porterhouse steak, the crackle of a crispy rice-flour crust on shrimp tempura—all of these elements, though not precisely what scientists would call taste—set up the actual palate experience that follows. Without texture, without touching and feeling, the most exquisite tastes are reduced to boring uniformity. This is yet another reason for the importance of mastering heat when you roast, sauté, braise, grill. With precise control of heat, you can determine the way your tongue first experiences the texture of the food you are preparing.

I should also mention something that often precedes texture: the "long distance" taste experience known as aroma. Sit in a dining room when the waiters shave a bulbous white truffle over a steaming risotto: the funky, almost sexy, aroma will reach you, quite powerfully, from fifty feet away. Up close it is as if you are wrapped in a truffle aura, a distillation of all the aromas of an autumn hillside in Alba—fermented wild berries, decaying oak leaves, musk of wild boar, smoky pine balsam.

Or to take a less rarefied (and less costly) example, think about a soup. What do you do when a hot bowl of soup is put in front of you? A chef will always *grab steam*, directing the wafts of vapor coming off, say, a prawn broth with accents of lemongrass, lime, leek and holy basil. You are wrapped up in a haze of anticipation and appetite even before anything hits your tongue.

So, taste is not a static thing. There is no simple, static Taste of Pike Quenelles in Nantua Sauce or Taste of Roasted Grouse in a Foamy Brown Butter with Cinnamon and Orange Peel. There is not even a simple Taste of Carrot. Instead, think of taste the way you experience a performance. Just as there is a beginning, middle and end to a play, there is a similar narrative to tasting. Usually taste starts with aroma, then moves to texture, then to the actual experience on the tongue, and finally, as you chew, swallow and breathe out, there is another waft of aroma that rises from your palate into your nostrils.

As a chef, you must be in control of all these elements and determine how strong and long lasting each of them will be. For example, rosemary on the olive oil-crisped skin of a freshly caught sea bass will wake up your palate right away then fade as the deeper yet subtle flavor of the bass develops. Yet I might want to lengthen that herbal taste on the palate, as I do with velvety pea soup topped with smooth rosemary and garlic-infused cream. Here the richness of the cream "spreads out" the pungent herb and garlic and extends the taste so that the relatively mild sweet pea picks up dimension and character.

Once you understand that there are many facets to the taste of each ingredient, you may overcome a common (usually fatal) tendency to achieve more flavor by complicating the recipe, adding more and more ingredients. Consider the endless variety, for instance, in the product of the winemaker's art. Although a great wine may combine a number of varietals in its "recipe," still wine has one major ingredient—the grape. But through the winemaker's labors, it expresses an infinite series of variations in the complex taste of wine.

Think about it. You can ferment cherries, apples, berries, plums, even cabbage. Theoretically one could create a beverage recipe by mixing various proportions of these juices, but who would want to drink it? Fermented grape juice, i.e. wine, offers more than enough

complexity. That is the point I am making with ingredients: not that it is bad to mix them in a recipe (indeed,
that is the basis of cooking), but that you add *only what it
is absolutely necessary*. For each ingredient you must have
an intimate knowledge of its *flavor profile*.

For example, we make a carrot coulis by sweating
very fresh, crisp carrots to concentrate their sweet flavor. Then we make a juice of raw carrots to preserve a
pristine fresh flavor. Then we blend the two and liven
up the mix with some lime that accents the fresh-from-
the-garden flavors of the carrot. Very simple. The one
extra ingredient—lime—effects a happy marriage of the
cooked and uncooked flavors, the sweet and tart. Of
course, spices and seasoning complete the process.

Or, in a more complex example, we make an apricot
custard tart with vanilla poached apricot purée. We top
the tart with fresh apricot coulis and serve it with a
baked apricot marmalade and almond ice cream, on top
of roasted apricot. Voila! Four different textures and
tastes of the apricot in one dish. Think of the cubist
paintings of Picasso or Braque: many views of the same
subject presented as one simultaneously. We are coaxing
layers of taste and surprises from one ingredient.

In considering specific tastes I start with salt, the
most fundamental aspect of seasoning. As I explained before, you may salt before you cook, while you cook and
as you plate. In each instance the salt does something a
little differently. At the beginning, it helps to draw tastes
to the surface, concentrating them. During the roasting,

salt helps to form an even more intense crust. Salt again when you remove it from the heat. Then, after the meat is sliced, a sprinkling of coarse salt on top pulls all the deep taste out of the meat while leaving little islands of crunchy salty texture that are even more concentrated.

A chef, you will have noticed by now, seasons and re-seasons, slowly adjusting the balance of taste. It used to be, when I started out, that the chef banned salt and pepper from the dining room, the implication being that the dish came from the kitchen perfectly seasoned. This may have been pleasing to the ego of the prima donna chef, but in fact all of us have different thresholds of taste, and what is undersalted to me might be just right for you. So, if asked to, we offer a little sea salt at table so that diners can make a final personal adjustment. Whatever you do, however, remember that *not* seasoning is not an option. While there may be people who need to restrict salt in-take, restaurants that cook with little or no seasoning cannot turn out great cuisine. Much better to go light on the salt on request than to subject all of your diners to the listless taste of unseasoned food.

And now to that bête noire of the High Priests of Lightness, butter. This wonderful ingredient has gotten a bum rap in my opinion, largely because some French chefs of the mid-twentieth century would add butter, cream and eggs to everything—hoping to accomplish through richness what they may have lacked in ingredients, technique or simply the time required for developing proper flavor.

To be sure, excess—in this case, of butter—is not a good thing. But in proportion, butter is most wonderful. Your clientele, for the most part, are not coming to a restaurant to eat a spa meal and then run off to a yoga class. They want to have their socks knocked off, gastronomically speaking. A little bit of butter goes a long way in this regard. Yes you can use olive oil or other more "heart healthy" oils for many of the things you do with butter, but the results will never be the same.

When we cook a piece of fish *Meuniere*, the heat of the lightly browned butter spooned over the flesh gently warms the insides and gives a nutty patina to the outside. The result is a combination of the flavor punch that fat in the form of foamy browned butter gives when properly used, a complex yet subtle transformation of the fish from a potentially bland filet of flounder to something spectacular. By the way, have you ever had a lobster poached in butter by Thomas Keller at the French Laundry? Ah, it is the best thing! The lobster has a delicate sweet flavor that poaching in butter at a low temperature enhances so that the taste is fresh-from-the-ocean. The curve of heating is not aggressive; rather, it is gradual primarily because the butter is well suited to this method of cooking, firming yet maintaining moisture.

Do not be a slave to the faddish idea that butter does not belong in the kitchen. Without it, you will never be able to cook so many of the recipes in the classique repertoire. From simple melted butter to beurre blanc to noisette to beurre noir, there is a wide spectrum to this versatile and delicious ingredient. So no, it is not something to resort to in order to add flavor when your culinary technique should have developed it in other ways, but yes, it is the pièce de résistance of so many recipes. Bear in mind that with popular modern techniques such as foaming (making a bubbly emulsion), butter does not have to equate with heavy. It works on much the same principle that allows just a little bit of milk to produce a rich frothy head on cappuccino that amplifies the coffee flavor. In a foam of butter and reduced stock, the bubbles in the emulsified butter allow it to cover more of the surface area of the taste buds, thereby delivering more taste with relatively less fat than Carême or Escoffier might have achieved with straight butter or cream. For example, I do a foamed *persillade* full of the clarity of parsley and headiness of garlic with which I lightly coat a roasted prawn set on crushed and truffled potatoes. The taste is powerful but the effect is light.

Now to the spice rack and herb garden. These elements can be subtle or overpowering. Their character and strength varies with the ingredients they accompany. For example, slide a sprig of tarragon between the skin and breast meat of a chicken and you will find a slightly anise and vanilla bouquet that will dominate the more delicate flesh. In a béarnaise, however, pickled tarragon becomes an accent. In my cooking—which, as I have said, is basically French—I rely on ten herbs or so to draw out the deeper layers of flavor in a dish. Some, such as basil and tarragon, have a certain licorice quality that dramatizes the sweetness in a dish.

Somewhat different in effect, oregano, thyme and sage help to frame and define more robust flavors. Take the example of a roast suckling pig. Its crisp fatty skin and succulent meat create a chorus of aroma and taste that can overwhelm the palate. Like air, which fills any container in which you put it, suckling pig will completely fill up every taste bud. To keep the taste in proportion to other elements of the meal, oregano, thyme and sage give shape and definition to taste, drawing out the most savory aspects.

Parsley and to an even greater degree watercress have two separate but complementary aspects. One accents freshness, while the other—somewhere between bitterness and peppery sharpness—helps to contain a taste and punctuate it (the way beer, for example, completely cleans off the palate and readies it for the next bite as if it were the first). In other words, rather than allowing flavor to accumulate and overwhelm, these herbs preserve the balance that otherwise could be tipped by a strong ingredient such as garlic. This is why in classical cooking parsley is often wedded to garlic, and fresh endive beds down cozily with Roquefort.

Ginger and lemongrass, though not true herbs, work to affect taste the way in which herbs do. These key ingredients in Southeast Asian cooking are in great danger of overuse, as they have essentially become the flavor of the month for fusion chefs. You must feel your way into these ingredients, because you do not have a lifetime of tasting experience with them going all the way back to childhood. I think of the brilliant former chef of Lespinasse, Gray Kunz, who dazzled New York diners all through the 1990s. Kunz grew up in Singapore, trained under Michelin-starred Fredy Girardet in Lausanne then worked in Hong Kong for five years. Kunz had French technique and an intimate knowledge of the Eastern palate. His walleye pike with lavender honey sauce or his rope mussels with lemongrass broth were examples of the finesse that comes from intimacy with ingredients, rather than a throw-it-all-in-the-pot-and-call-it-exotic approach of many modern chefs who like the idea of fusion cooking but who have not rigorously studied it.

For myself, I like to imagine the taste of a new ingredient then build from there. For example, I wanted to make a chilled velouté for oyster that would be creamy and briny, with subtle, unexpected, almost unidentifiable undertones. So I combined cream, chicken stock and gelatin, and infused the mixture with coriander seeds, lime peel, ginger, keffir lime leaves and lemongrass. So floral and fragrant. Set an oyster afloat in it and you have a fusillade of the lightest, subtly complex tastes. I pick up the scent of the seacoast taste of Brittany alongside the mystery and delicacy of the East.

Aromatic spices such as cloves, cumin, anise, curry (this last is actually a mix of spices) also frame tastes beautifully as well as helping them punch through. Certain meats accept aromatics very well: pork, for example, and chicken (especially white meat). Aromatics give an instant identity to recipes, but as with everything, only in proportion. They can also overwhelm with their strong perfume and slightly acrid taste. The East and Middle East are as famous for their aromatic spice mixes as are the French for their sauces. That is where your world tour serves you well.

As I mentioned earlier, my global tour as a young chef pretty much began and ended in Denmark when Vergé sent me there to work at the Plaza Hotel in Copenhagen. Still, even this limited travel broadened me. I was captivated by Danish butter, bacon and hams. Also aromatic cumin, caraway, rye seed and dill seed. These are extremely good in marinades. The one big development in my cuisine was my sense of cumin, an aromatic that really hits you with the first bite. But then its impact grows less noticeable until finally it recedes into the overall flavor of a recipe. In Mexico or Kerala I would also have come across cumin, but in those cornucopia of spices I might not have developed the more complete understanding of cumin that I got in Denmark.

How you season or use butter or herbs and spices are the signatures of a chef, but they are of little use without the best ingredients. Finding the best and coaxing all the flavor out of them are subjects that I will explore in my next letter.

INGREDIENTS

There can never be—has never been—a great restaurant with second-class ingredients. Whether it is as common as lettuce or as rarefied as white truffles or sushi-quality tuna, you must seek out the best. If you find yourself working for a chef who uses second-class ingredients, get out of there.

Of course, like everything else, pride in one's ingredients can be taken to extremes. In France, when I was young, there was a chef by the name of Thuilier. He was famous for his pride and for his volcanic temper. One day, the story goes, he was making the rounds in his dining room and a patron complimented him on a wonderful dish but added, "It's too bad you couldn't find fresh green beans."

Incensed, Thuilier stormed into the kitchen, grabbed a whole crate of beautiful fresh green beans, went back into the dining room and emptied the entire contents on the table of the complaining diner. "Get out of my restaurant!" the chef ordered. "And do not ever come here again."

Thuilier was over the top, but his point is well taken. A great chef will not serve inferior ingredients. It follows, then, that a great chef will always seek out the best ingredients. Even if you have your own farm, a fishing boat and a platoon of hunters in the fields, you won't be able to grow fruits in winter or find truffles in spring, catch shad in the summer or pick ramps in the fall. In other words, any chef is dependent on the seasons and his suppliers. A great supplier is as driven in his or her pursuit of the best as any great chef is. *Purveyors*, to use the term more common among chefs, are our connection to quality. Find these people and treat them like family. Feed them when they come to you. Send some cakes and cookies home for their kids. Spend time with them discussing their passion (that is, your ingredients).

A number of the top restaurants in New York get their poultry from a tiny dynamo of a woman named Sylvie Pryzant and her husband, Steve, a native of Manhattan's Yorkville. Though Sylvie's story is unusual, it is typical of many suppliers in that it is about arriving at a calling in life. She is a Tunisian Jew who was forced to leave her homeland in 1963. After passing her youth in Paris, she went to Israel where she met her husband on a kibbutz. It proved difficult for her and Steve to get their own farm in Israel, so they came to the States and bought themselves a farm in Pennsylvania about three hours from Midtown Manhattan. They went into the business raising snow-white milk-fed veal. But they had absolutely no connections in the restaurant business.

That was no obstacle to Sylvie. She picked up the phone and called every top chef in town, until one of them (Tom Colicchio at Gramercy Tavern) returned her call, tried her veal and became a customer. With veal, Sylvie and Steve soon found that it is a long time between paychecks (it takes three months to raise a calf), so they decided to go into the milk-fed poultry business. There was only one problem. Nobody in America raised milk-fed poultry (which meant, in turn, that we chefs could never serve those wonderful *poulets de Bresse* that we had in France). But Sylvie was obsessed and would not stop until she learned the secret of the Bresse chicken, so she called Georges Blanc (my former mentor) in France and said, "Chef, what is the secret to raising these chickens?" Guess what? Blanc actually told her how to gradually change the chicken's diet from grain to milk pellets. Within a year, the top New York restaurants were serving milk-fed capon and their younger versions, the poularde and poussin.

Moral of the story: one Sylvie and one Steve Pryzant are worth 2,000 everyday chicken farmers. So if you meet people who talk about the ingredients they offer with the same fond smile that others save for anecdotes about their children, get to know them. Try their product and if it is good, treasure the people as you treasure the ingredients.

Another example is my friend Rod Mitchell. He comes from generations of Maine fishermen. His first career, though, was in the wine business where he met Jean Louis Palladin, the superb French chef who brought me to America. It was Jean Louis who convinced Rod that there was a market for hand-harvested divers scallops. Rod was the first person I heard of to offer these succulent, super fresh and sweet morsels. On a visit to Maine, Jean Louis, acting on a hunch, took a net down to the river and hauled in some small eels (*piballes*), one of the favorite fish ingredients of the southwest of France. With no bones to speak of, they are an unforgettable delicacy with nothing more than espelette peppers, olive oil and garlic. Rod took up Jean Louis's challenge and began to supply French restaurants with baby American eels, something we might never have had were it not for a friendship between chef and supplier.

Of course, Rod's seafood sometimes costs more than regular fish from the Fulton Fish Market. But it is not surprising. He gets me wild Copper River salmon in the summer, as deeply pink as lobster coral. Closer to home he finds silvery striped bass, fresh skate, halibut, cod . . . the best of the ocean. These things too cost more, which brings me to another important point: *Buy the best ingredients you can afford.*

Basically, there have been two cuisines where the price of ingredients has not been a controlling factor: French and Japanese. In Paris you can charge $100 for a main course and, if you are Guy Savoy, you may have a full house every night. In Japan you can have a little ten-seat sushi house on the Inland Sea and charge enough to keep two fishing boats working full time to find you the tuna with the best *toro*, the prized mackerel known as *aji*, plump live shrimp.

With those cuisines, as with yours, clientele and imagination determine what ingredients you should buy and can afford to buy. It does not all have to be truffles, foie gras and caviar. It can be blood-red heirloom tomatoes, hand-foraged field greens, crisp October apples. Still, for a great restaurant you will occasionally have to shell out for the expensive stuff. Just find a way to be sure you can sell it and that you use every shaving of truffle, every last caviar egg, every slice of foie gras. Waste is always the restaurateur's enemy, doubly so when the ingredients are as expensive as gold (last year I paid $1,400 a pound for Italian white truffles!).

In the end, cost is not what determines quality—nature and seasons do. Although we live in an age when you can pretty much get any ingredient you want year round, for most of our history on this planet we have evolved to be hungry for foods in their season.

I grew up on a farm where we ate what we grew. It could not have been more seasonal. For nine months of the year we never ate a zucchini, but when they were in season, we made something with them almost every day. In fall, we had crisp tart apples and sweet musky pears that we stored under the top couple of inches of barley in our silo. The fruits would slowly ripen and keep for three months, well into the winter. So yes, we did eat them "out of season," I suppose, but we preserved them at their peak of flavor.

It is their very peakness that makes seasonality so important to ingredients. Spring is the wakening earth, summer its sweet season, fall a time of ripeness. All of us, not just chefs, can't help but think this way. Seen in this light, ingredients connect us in the most basic way to the rhythm of the planet.

When a new season comes, I return to my favorite dishes for that time of year, but I find it is also a time to challenge oneself to create new dishes. That is one of the lovely mysteries of cuisine, how seeing an ingredient for the first time each year somehow spurs one to create. Listen to your inner chef; it will tell you that the fava beans before you need a baby carrot coulis alongside some poached crayfish. Or it will tell you that a gnarly Hubbard squash in the market is incomplete until filled with black walnuts, fennel sausage, Macoun apples and a lacing of Calvados.

There was a time when I believed that the best ingredients (and therefore the only ones worth using) were those that could be trucked in. In Lyon, in my boyhood, this was certainly true. Within driving distance, the fruit and vegetables would ripen in the fields and orchards and be at their absolute peak. The fish would be a few hours from the sea, the cheeses just a day's drive from the aging caves in the mountains.

For the most part, I still like to cook that way. To be sure, I can get amazing cherries from Chile in December. By the same token, I can also go swimming in a heated pool in New York in December—but somehow neither the swimming nor the cherries seem connected with the season, and for that reason I find them out of place.

I am not above "pushing" the seasons a little bit, getting peaches from the Carolinas in June or Florida tomatoes at that time. The suppliers load them up on an eighteen wheeler—hot from the orchard or field—and we have them three days later, beautifully ripe. Or I can call my mushroom supplier from Oregon and have chanterelles picked one day and in my prep kitchen the next. Because of modern transportation, then, these foods are still seasonal—at their peak—and still have a relation to the season in New York.

In the modern larder not everything is local, so I do not always need to feel a seasonal connection to cook with these ingredients. Passion fruits are completely exotic to me, so I can cook with them any time of the year and not feel that I am breaking my connection to the season. I used to feel this way about pineapples, but in recent years we have begun to see golden Hawaiian pineapples that are tender and fairly bursting with juice. Now I tend to wait on cooking with pineapples until I see the golden ones in the market.

In addition to fruits and vegetables, fish, fowl and meat have seasons as well. Again, I try to stay in tune with my local season or at least the spirit of the season. Spring lamb from the hills of eastern Pennsylvania, Gardiners Bay scallops in October, shad from the Hudson in May, Scottish grouse in August, Delaware duck and goose in the fall, upstate New York venison in early winter.

If you are in tune with the seasons, you will dream about cooking with a particular ingredient when you can find it readily in the market. Stay with the seasons and you cannot go wrong. You will be, as the saying goes, "happy as God in France." And if you have ever been in a French market full of the choice offerings of the season—bounteous, exploding with flavor, a palette of deep colors to inspire an artist—you will understand why God is so happy. P.S. These days, when I consider ingredients, I think God could be pretty happy in Barcelona, Tuscany and upstate New York too.

■ WINE AND PASTRY

Let's consider economics. When you have your own restaurant and start to review your accounting, you will see that savory foods—the items that come from the garde-manger, or the meat and fish lines—account for a little bit more than half the average check. About 10 to 15 percent of that check is generated by the pastry department, and nearly one-third goes to the wine cellar. So it is absolutely critical that the complete chef be very conversant with wine and pastry.

Let's take those economics a bit further. Although wine is just 30 percent of the business, the profit margin on it is often much higher, sometimes double the profit on food. This is not, as many people think, because we mark up the bottles two or three hundred percent. The important thing is to invest in wines that are relatively inexpensive when they are released but that will become more and more valuable as the years go by. For example, our wine director Jean Luc Le Dû bought some Château

Latour 2000 for approximately $200 per bottle. One year later, that bottle might cost $300. Still later, at fair market price we may expect to charge $900 in 2007 for it—that is, a yearly compounded rate of interest of 24 percent . . . just by choosing a good wine and holding on to it. Actually, it will be a little bit less because there is no guarantee that a bottle will not be corked. You must also figure in capital costs, the price of storage, interest foregone had you left the money in the bank, and god forbid a bottle be knocked off the shelf as a frantic waiter hurries to satisfy a demanding customer. And, finally, there is always the risk of what happens should the economy tank.

The restaurant mark-up on wine is indeed greater than the liquor store's, but wine has to carry more costs in a fine dining restaurant. Basically, the profit margin on food is minimal, so the crystal, the flower arrangements, the beautiful china that one expects in a fine dining restaurant have to be paid for by something. By long tradition, patrons have shown a willingness to pay for those extras in the wine tab.

A great wine list will attract a great clientele, one that knows the value of wine and is willing to indulge. The quality of your wine list will bear a direct and significant impact on your average check in two ways. The wine itself contributes directly to the check. Moreover, the diner who will pay gladly for a Haut Brion or Château Margaux will expect only the finest ingredients—the truffles, the grouse, the wild salmon, the porcini. The decision to buy these luxury ingredients in affordable quantities means you will have enough so that you can also offer them to the folks who are buying the less costly bottle of wine.

Vintage Bordeaux represents the big time in collectibles and investment. Then there is Burgundy, the premium Italians and American cult wines close behind. So you must have a list that represents these categories. While it is important for a gastronomic restaurant to have that Latour '61 for the customer who wants the best and does not care about price, it is just as important for your reputation to have newer, lesser known winemakers and less costly bottles. For example, I take greater pride in finding some of Jim Clendenen's impeccable 2001 Au Bon Climat, Bien Nacido than in buying a '78 Corton, which is already well known to every oenophile. Someday the young producers are going to become the old masters, and, of equal importance, you will have diners who want good wine but do not have the pocketbook to go for the pricey stuff.

Those customers are your future and you cannot afford to drive them away with the sticker shock of a Greatest Hits wine list.

As a young chef you will have many opportunities to broaden your knowledge of wine. These days, there are tastings all around town (not only New York, but any serious restaurant town). There also is a tremendous depth of information in books, newspapers and magazines. Still, there is no substitute for tasting. Just watch how much you taste. I remember at one of my early jobs, we had one old chef—a good chef at that—who was pretty lit five days out of six. That will not fly anymore.

You have advantages that I didn't when I started. Being French, we accepted wine as part of life, but if we had to drive somewhere to get it, my dad's philosophy was, Why bother? Like most Frenchmen, we drank the wine of our region, northern Rhônes and southern Burgundies: for me, thick, sun-rich Syrah, crisp, delicate yet powerful Pinot Noir. It wasn't until I worked in a fancy restaurant in Lyon that I began to learn about Bordeaux. Where the bold and brawny Burgundies and Rhônes of my youth were a pure expression of *terroir* (the land, the climate and the *je ne sais quois* that defines a wine region), Bordeaux often has more elegance and lightness.

At my next job, at Georges Blanc, on our days off we would try the wine of Maconnais and Beaujolais, regional wines such as those of Provence and the Loire, good for the table and affordable, very representative of the wide range of wines in the French bistro tradition. We would visit winemakers, have wine at lunch and, to tell the truth, by five in the afternoon we were feeling toasty. But we were young, and that is the way young chefs were (and still are).

From those years I came away with the conviction that a great gastronomic restaurant requires a great wine list, and a regular restaurant wants good everyday wines. *En français* we say, *grand restaurant et grand vin, petit restaurant et petit vin.* No value judgment here but still true in the global setting. White tablecloths versus bare wooden tables: both charming but different.

At my restaurants, we encourage kitchen staff to join the waiters and attend classes on wine, or to come to tastings directed by the sommeliers. I will see those same faces at wine tastings that I see bent over their notebooks jotting down recipes in the kitchen, or spending their down time asking other cooks about ingredients, techniques and so on. It boils down to this: The young chef who has ambitions to be a great chef is interested in every aspect of the business, and wine is a very big aspect.

Apart from being a companion to food, wine is a primary ingredient in French cuisine. It is fundamental in Italian, German, Spanish and modern American cooking too. Wine helps to balance acidity and concentrate and enrich flavor in a way that vinegar or lemon juice or beer cannot. Only wine has the complexity to bring out the length of flavor in a ribeye steak à la bordelaise sauce or a *civet de lapin* or *poularde* in a creamy Riesling sauce.

Finally, there is something magical about wine that I cannot put into words. Perhaps wine is sacramental because it is touched with an aura of the mystical and sacred. Certainly the French treat it that way. I remember my parents telling me stories of the war when every family hid their wine from the enemy. The invaders could take other things, but *never* would they take our wine! From the great châteaux of Bordeaux to the hills of Côte Rôtie and even in my own home, wine was hidden with the family jewels. My grandfather, Joseph Boulud, dug a secret underground bunker to hide our wine. In our case, it was not about the value of the wine to collectors but rather the value of the wine as something the family held and loved in common. Wine was part of our patrimony. In part, it is what has made us French.

Wine, then, is the essence of the French dining experience. So are the wonderful sugary caprices that pour out of the pastry kitchen, although there are no stories of families hiding treasure troves of pastry in their cellars. Everybody loves pastry and even the most diet-conscious diners usually give in and have something rich and sweet for dessert. They do not do this every night at home, but when they come to a fine restaurant they usually think, "Why not? One pear clafoutis won't push me up three dress sizes."

Gastronomically, dessert is important. The palate craves sweetness at the end of a meal. There is something warm and cozy about dessert, like a goodnight kiss from mom before she would tuck you in at night. That childhood craving that stays with grown-up diners will account for 10 to 15 percent of the check. Although food costs for desserts are relatively low (flour, sugar, butter), labor costs—especially if you have an "artistic" dessert chef—run high. Still, I believe it is worthwhile to have a high-ticket pastry chef because well-conceived, well-executed, well-marketed desserts can be twice as profitable as your main courses and appetizer. That is a huge hunk of business, one that you cannot afford to leave to the printed menu and hope that the customer takes the hint. These days, when everyone is counting calories and many share desserts, you need to reawaken people's appetites with a special dessert menu while making sure that your wait staff is trained in describing the sweets in the most tantalizing manner.

For your own foundation as a chef, you must acquire an understanding of baking (both bread and pastry). It is much easier to do this when you are younger rather than waiting until the responsibilities of the kitchen pile up on you. Just like the young chef who comes to our wine tastings, the young chef who spends an afternoon every now and then with the pastry chef or bread baker is the person I recognize as having the drive and ambition to advance in this business.

Although pastry and the rest of the menu both come out of the kitchen and all are made by a brigade in checked pants and white coats, they are two very different disciplines. Cooking is all about speed and creativity in technique. It is also about the ability to improvise, to accommodate variations in ingredients, while maintaining consistency in the finished product. Pastry is the opposite. It is less about spontaneous creativity and more about precision and measuring. Instead of speed, it is about waiting. Pastry ingredients—flour, sugar, butter, sometimes chocolate—are much more uniform than the basic ingredients in appetizers and main courses. In a way, pastry is more like chemistry, whereas the rest of cooking is rather like music. Both have a written-out plan, but in baking you rarely deviate and in cooking you often must change and adapt. Classical versus jazz, if you will.

The creativity of the pastry chef often expresses itself in outlandish presentation and delicious combinations. If, as they say, first impressions are important, last impressions are equally so in a restaurant. It is hard for the customer to forget a *mille-feuille* (literally translated as a thousand sheets) of parchment-thin sheets of extra bitter Venezuelan chocolate separating wafers of toasted hazelnut praline, held together by multilevels of pillowy soft Arabica coffee mousse and crowned with a zabaglione of smoky Kentucky bourbon. Crunchy, toasty, bitter, sweet, mildly intoxicating and thoroughly seductive.

You may never be a pastry chef, but you cannot even call yourself a chef at all if you have not mastered the art of making dough. It is basic to desserts, but also to many of the things we do with hot and cold appetizers as well as with main courses. For example, brioche, pâté sablée and puff pastry are used as much in savory items as in sweets. Crayfish, morels, sweetbreads and asparagus in a foamy chervil sauce on a flaky golden pastry crust is a far cry from a tart of crushed fresh figs tossed with cinnamon and brown sugar and baked over a butter-rich crust. Still, they both depend on mastering the delicate and demanding art of puff pastry. So, even though you may have little interest in becoming a pastry chef because you have your sights set on the line, some time on the dough station will serve you well.

Did you ever watch a pastry chef draw a picture of a dessert? It is almost like watching an architect. You are struck with the physical design, how flavor is located in different layers, the way texture enters into the equation. Where a line cook might rely more on gut and inspiration, the pastry chef always plans it out. Many line cooks I have known would have benefited from this kind of planning. No doubt I have such respect for the pastry chef because Michel Guérard, as well as Michel Richard of Citronelle in Washington, D.C., were both pastry chefs before they decided to become chef chefs. Their visual artistry, by virtue of their pastry background, is beyond the capability of most traditional, nonpastry chefs.

While I can think of nothing more perfect than a classic chocolatey and creamy éclair washed down with a cup of espresso, at the same time, I will never say no to some just-invented passion fruit extravaganza topped with a scoop of saffron gelato. One is not better than the other, and whether you want to create traditional or original desserts you must understand the basic principles of pastry and desserts as they are practiced by pastry chefs. Then you must learn to let your imagination go.

For example, I mentioned earlier how I am interested in exploring all the facets of the flavor profile of an ingredient. Right now we are making a strawberry, lime and rhubarb dessert. In a glass, layer a light lime gelée, a mix of fresh and stewed strawberries, a tart lime whipped cream with strawberry granita and rhubarb ice cream. Alongside we place a warm rhubarb turnover. Three basic ingredients (rhubarb, lime and strawberry) presented in a multitude of ways.

Without knowledge of how to use sugar precisely, how to create sweetened creams, how to layer elements, this would be a messy dessert, the kind that kids make when they dump every sweet thing in the refrigerator into a mixing bowl. Only by virtue of the fact that we have studied the science of sweetness and pastry as well as basic cuisine can we get to an interesting and novel "chef's dessert." And if there is ever a place where pure whimsy and caprice rule on the menu, it is in the desserts.

■ THE GRAND TOUR

Experiencing other cuisines on their home territory is more important today, in the era of fusion, than it ever was. I think it will be even more so in the future. But before you buy your tickets and take off for Bangkok, there are some things you need to ask yourself.

First, what kind of food interests you? Italian, French, Chinese, Mexican, Indian, Thai, Japanese? If you have an idea of what you particularly like, often this is an indication of what you ought to see and try. You do not always have to travel the world, by the way. In New York City, you could sample at least thirty different cuisines—in true ethnic communities—if you hopped the Number 7 train at Grand Central and got off at every stop in Queens. You will find restaurants, groceries, butchers, bakers, fish stores, all specializing in ethnic ingredients.

New York is not America's only melting pot. San Francisco, New Orleans, Los Angeles, Seattle, Houston, all have ethnic communities: Vietnamese, Italian, Mexican, Japanese, Polish, Portuguese. So you can do a lot of your world traveling close to home. The important thing is that you try the real thing—true cuisines—wherever you can find them.

Even for the explorer who does not have access to the real thing, we are all floating on a sea of cookbooks and magazines crammed with recipes of different world cuisines. The Wednesday dining section of the *New York Times* (or the food section of any metropolitan paper), if you read it for a year, will pretty much take you around the world.

We did not have such a wide exposure to global cuisine when I was a young chef. And truth to tell, we didn't think we needed it. I understand why we thought that way. We were French, and the French all think that haute cuisine is French Cuisine. French is the language of haute cuisine the way English is the international language of air traffic control.

I have since come to learn things are not that simple, but at the same time, the modern restaurant is a French invention; the "software"—that is, the way a restaurant is organized—is likewise French. And nowhere else have chefs taken a national cuisine and refined it so much and as variedly as have the French. Part of the explanation is that France in the latter part of the eighteenth century was the first country to develop true restaurants: a varied bill of fare, set prices, the ability to order a la carte. As restaurants developed, a culture evolved with them. Cuisine held a rank alongside theater and the other arts. The result was a public that would pay the price for haute cuisine and challenge their chefs to new heights of creativity.

The French took dining, a part of daily life, raised it to an art, embedded it in high culture and thereby attracted the economic resources to develop a more refined and expert interpretation of food than anywhere else in the world. In much the same way, French haute couture took another part of daily life and similarly developed it. A dress embroidered with pearls and trimmed with fur is, in some sense, not unlike a saddle of veal studded with truffles, stuffed with chestnuts and glazed with port. It is expensive. It is refined. But it would never happen were it not for a public that appreciated and would pay for it. Cultures make choices for their definitive statements. The Italians lavished everything on developing their opera and the Russians their ballet. The French chose haute cuisine and haute couture. Today these two *hautes* have globalized, yet kept their French sensibility.

Even in France, however, chefs have learned to include North African and Indochinese culinary traditions (one of the very few good results of colonialism). When Alain Senderens made his reputation as one of the most innovative chefs in the nouvelle cuisine movement, he had a young Cambodian in the kitchen, Sottha Khun (my good friend and former executive chef at Le Cirque), who could tell him if the new Asian flavors he was trying rang true. I do not know where Senderens got his inspiration for combining lobster and vanilla bean, but it certainly came from outside the canon of French cuisine. It was one of the defining recipes of nouvelle cuisine and I suspect it came out of the fact that with all the international influences included in his food, he was open to the strangest yet most wonderful combinations.

The Lyonnais regarded themselves as residents of the world's food capital when I started out. Even if you didn't agree with them, you could see why they thought this. If you drew a ring around Lyon fifty miles from Place Bellecour, you would probably encircle more Michelin stars than anywhere in the world, including Paris. So the grand tour of the world's cuisines was not such a big thing with us.

Still, after a short while in the business, I yearned to see something new, anything. So, when I was sixteen, I told Nandron that I wanted to take a summer vacation. Like a true French chef, his answer was, "You do not need a vacation, for God's sake, you are sixteen years old! I'll get you a job at my friend's auberge in the Pays Basque."

So I left my home region for the first time and worked for three months at a restaurant in the most remote corner of southwestern France (in the Hotel Etchola in the little village of Ascain). Same country, but what a revelation! The trout just about jumped into your bucket from the mountain streams of the Pyrénées. There were the heavenly pungent cheeses from goats and sheep that grazed on sweet mountain grasses! And the *Jambon de Bayonne* and wild mushrooms and invigorating Espelette peppers were all new and exciting to me. I immediately learned the importance to a young chef of being open to other cuisines. *Hybrid vigor* is the term used in agriculture to describe how the offspring of two genetic strains is often more robust than either parent; the same is true in cooking.

If I were your age, I would think about a trip to France, Spain or Italy—those are the three richest European cuisines to my way of thinking. Eat everywhere you can. Go to the markets, the wineries, the shops. If you can find a position, then by all means get a *stage* or cook's job for six months.

Or pay attention to your family's traditions. In the United States, of course, we have a vibrant Italian community. I am sure that his Italian roots helped form the culinary style of Andrew Carmellini, the executive chef at Café Boulud. From childhood he has loved simple rustic gnocchi. You can have them in many Italian restaurants—but not with lemon and caviar as he makes gnocchi for our customers. My real point is that coming at things through the focus of culinary tradition allows you to create with confidence.

Apart from Europe and its culinary offsprings in the states, India and Mexico both offer varied cuisines, tremendous refinement and novel (to a European palate) ways of combining flavors and textures. China, too, has a rich culinary tradition and I would love to visit there. Its imperial cuisine did for the native cuisine what French gastronomy did for our home cuisines.

Peru has wonderful ceviches and with the large Japanese population wonderful sushi as well: You could not think of a better place to learn about raw fish and marinades than Peru. Argentina has a reputation for the best meat in the world and they are master grillers.

The cuisines of the Middle East are as rich as any, with a sophisticated use of aromatic spices. Then, of course, there is Vietnamese food, for which we French chefs have a special fondness. Before the word *fusion* had anything to do with food, French chefs were marrying their techniques with the ingredients and recipes of this ancient and elegant cuisine. The result was a multicultural cuisine of depth and refinement.

Any place in Indochina—Thailand, Laos, Burma— will offer you a great cooking tradition with more exotic-looking fruits and vegetables and more varied seafood than you would have thought possible: and the region is so sensual with its spices, flowers, temples and tropical air.

Take six months to two years. Travel the world, work with chefs everywhere you can, eat every kind of food. And then get ready for the rude awakening when you return home and begin a job at a top restaurant. It could be mine or Alfred Portale's Gotham Bar and Grill or Mark Miller's Coyote Café in Santa Fe or Thomas Keller's French Laundry in the Napa valley. Nobody is going to care all that much that you have been to Italy or Singapore or Shanghai because their main concern is only how well you can cook their food. They'll look at your resume, check your references, look you in the eye and if you are lucky, they will hire you. When that happens, your immediate task in life is no longer to dream about fusion and faraway temples. What matters now is the clatter and heat of a real kitchen and a chef who wants it his way.

So nourish your culinary soul with a world tour when you have the chance and continue to nourish it with Sunday trips to restaurants or trying out new cookbooks. Frankly, you may not have the time or pocketbook that let you travel and take jobs here and there, but you can still let your imagination roam. This will give you greater perspective as a chef and will somehow seep into your ideas and techniques when you get the chance.

Fantasy world versus real world: this is the dichotomy customers make when they choose your restaurant for a night. And fantasy world versus real world is what keeps us all going in the kitchen when the orders back up, tempers flare, waiters mix up their tables, soufflés fall . . . you name it.

Soak up all you can about this fantasy world now; then it is time to start building your career.

DESIRE, DRIVE
AND DISCIPLINE

I had a young chef come to me the other day who had been doing a great job at garde-manger. He wanted to move onto the line as a cook, which is pretty true to form for any aspiring chef. So we moved him to *poissonier* (the fish station) and right away you could see his lack of experience, speed and productivity. He had to go back to square one. Mind you, his would be a very good square one but we would have to watch over him, to use the French phrase, *comme le lait sur le feu*—like milk on the fire. In other words, we would have to watch him very carefully to make sure he did not suddenly upset the entire service by overcooking, oversalting, charring, forgetting an ingredient or making other errors in technique and method that can ruin a recipe as quickly as an unwatched pan of milk can boil over.

For him to master the simple technique of controlling heat on the stovetop will take time. As many restaurants do, we have a series of metal rings that cover each burner: By moving the pot closer to or further from that heat epi-center, you can get heat that is over 800° or as low as a lazy simmer. This young chef will get the hang of it. If he has talent and is driven, the day will come in the not too distant future when he can master the heat.

Just be prepared for the chef to throw you a curve. They all do. When I had maybe a year under my belt at my first job, my boss, after a week of hunting in Alsace, arrived with his Citroen DS 21 (the French Cadillac), opened the trunk and it was full of game. Pheasants, hares, partridge, woodcock. All were going on the menu for that night and I had to get them ready for service. Two other guys and I spent the whole afternoon plucking birds, dressing them, and for that evening learning six new recipes to create a wild game feast. I had cooked game that my family and I had shot my whole life; but now, in a seri-ous restaurant, new combinations of ingredients were coming at me from every direction. We had pheasant ter-rine, partridge au choux, woodcock flambé a l'Armagnac with croutons spread with crushed woodcock giblets and butter. And *lièvre à la royale*—boneless wild hare stuffed with foie gras truffles and ground pork, braised till spoon tender in a concentrated red wine and hare stock. So much to learn and do so fast. I had to run like crazy to stay up with the service and not make any mistakes.

Of course, these kinds of surprises are not the rule. Most restaurant work is endless repetition of simple techniques. Let me give you an idea of the day you can look forward to at one of my restaurants or Danny Meyer's or Susan Spicer's or Wolfgang Puck's—it doesn't matter whose, because the work is the same. Let's say you are at my restaurant, Daniel. We do not do lunch there, so if you are a cook, you will come in late morning and may stay until late at night.

Sometime in the next ten hours you can count on me or the sous-chef or whoever is above you to get on your case pretty hard. Get used to it. The time you have to worry is when I am not constantly on your case. I wouldn't waste my time if I didn't think you had something going for you. That's probably small consolation when you're getting chewed out for overcooking a halibut, but in all honesty that's about as close as you'll ever get to winning a medal in my kitchen. Praise in a kitchen is the absence of criticism.

Through the course of the day you'll have a couple of breaks and a meal or two, but between 1:00 and 5:30 you are getting prepared, doing your *mise-en-place*. If you have talent, discipline, speed and focus, you will get through this quickly. If you are new on the station, you may have discipline and focus, but there is no way that you can work at the same pace as an experienced chef. In that event, you will need to start earlier because it will take time to get up to speed. We will give you the drill of what you have to do and how you should do it—how to shell a pea very quickly, how to debone a squab rapidly, how to mince shallots into microdice, but then your level of skill and preplanning takes over.

I had one prep cook, Chepe, who could go through three cases of peas by the time a young cook had done a pound. I do not expect the young cook to be as quick as Chepe. I cannot even describe how he does it. It is one of those things experts do in a blur of hands and a pile of pods. But a smart young cook, when given the job, would watch Chepe for a while, then put his or her observations to work.

Skill and planning ahead take practice. Every skill takes practice, including the skill of knowing how much you have to do. Though you may have the technical aspects of *mise-en-place* down, if you have not figured out how much is required, you will either waste time or mess up the smooth flow of service by doing too much or too little prep. Wasted motion in the kitchen has a time cost, often as disruptive as insufficient preparation. By looking at the reservations, the number of portions available, the semipredictable habits of the clientele, you should know exactly what you need to do to be ready.

Doing all of these things correctly in the midst of the many demands of a first-rate kitchen requires aggressiveness, concentration and most of all, stamina. Your job is not merely to get through this pile of onions or that particular garnish—your job is to work rapidly *with precision*.

In prep or service we do not have time to slow down, so the only way to get up to speed is to invest your free time in honing your skill, spending time with the men and women who are the best at each particular task.

Then, as you concentrate and practice, it gets easier and you can relax. This is not to say that the work gets easier, but the pressure lifts as you become more accomplished and organized, planning your day according to what you need to get done and the level of your ability—always remembering that in addition to the one task you are trying to master there are five or six others that you will be called upon to finish at the same time!

I remember in Vergé's kitchen having to prep *mousseron* mushrooms and baby artichokes on the same morning. Both were included in popular items on the menu, so there were mountains of them. The baby artichokes required force, speed and a well-balanced knife hand to peel away the tough outer layers. It was a mean job. The tiny cap mushrooms, though, required more delicacy and a lighter touch to trim the stem. Two different skills, neither of them ones you naturally possess just by picking up a knife. I can still hear Vergé's direction to his troops, which comprised his entire employee motivation scheme: *Plus vite, encore plus vite*. Faster, and then even faster. But I was doing it as fast as I could.

So the bottom line is, the only way you will advance in this profession is if you invest your own time over and above your time on the clock. If you are driven to be a chef, this will not be an issue. I suppose the same is true for orchestra conductors, race car drivers, law professors and ballerinas. Every profession that draws ambitious dreamers demands time. It will come naturally to you because your interest and your desire will constantly propel you to the kitchen. And when you are done with your current task, you will be peppering the sous-chef on the next station with questions. You can't help it. It is in your blood. It does not make the time commitment easier or leave you any less tired at the end of the day, but people who are driven by something—or better yet, drawn irresistibly to a goal—do not count being tired as a bad thing.

When the day comes that you have mastered one station, your chef will move you to another one. Hopefully, it will not come as a complete novelty because you have been interested and observant about the rest of the kitchen. Still, when you have to take on the next job, you will start all over again, knowing next to nothing and not even doing that particularly well. But if you put in the time and have the desire, you will learn and we will teach you.

You must look inside yourself and find desire, because if you have it then you will make the time sacrifices and endure the criticism. Although I will never deny that it is hard work to become a chef, the clatter of the kitchen, the intense aromas, the mix of languages, the precision teamwork of the kitchen brigade when the service is really rocking . . . all of these things make me feel alive and charged in a way that nothing else can. So yes, you work until you are bone tired, but there is nothing else you would rather do. Is that any different from a tennis player who wants to make it to Wimbledon or a violinist whose ambition is the Philharmonic?

One more requirement—you need youth. Notice these are Letters to a *Young* Chef, not a new chef. In other words, if you were thirty years old I would not be writing this to you, because the demands of the job and the competition out there require that you start young, as you have, as I did. Though as I write this advice, I remember that Thuilier, whose volcanic temper I described earlier, was a successful insurance broker in Paris until, at age fifty, he moved down south and opened Les Baux de Provence. But he is the exception. Since he lived into his eighties, he had as long a run as a top chef (three-star Michelin) as anyone in the business.

But back to you, my young friend. Every newcomer I have ever known who then went on to become an accomplished chef kept a diary of techniques and recipes and a small collection of "holy books." I still have my tattered copy of Gringoire and Saulnier's *Le Répertoire de la Cuisine*, which was my version of CliffsNotes for cooks, full of the basics of recipes and definitions of terms. If the chef asked me to cut something *paysanne* style, instead of scratching my head and wondering how on earth a peasant would cut things, I looked it up in *Le Répertoire* and found that it means large rustic slices.

Being obsessed with the world of the chef brings me to the subject of pride in one's craft. Such pride comes across first in your appearance. If you look crisp and clean, that tells me you have respect for your profession. If I go into a kitchen and see lots of messy, sloppy chefs, it makes me think that they have the same attitude toward cuisine and service. America is a casual country and kitchens can sometimes get an overly laid back look and feel. In my mind there is nothing laid-back about a first-class kitchen. I would no more expect to see shorts and ponytails in a great kitchen then I would expect to see the New York Baroque Ensemble play in tee shirts. Of course, if you have made it to the level where you are a proven talent and want to make a statement with your image, like Mario Batali, I have no problem with that.

For example, I had one pastry chef, Johnny Iuzzini, who worked with me for seven years (he is now with Jean-Georges Vongerichten). He was great. He had energy, talent, creativity, and he was a leader. When he started to come to work with green hair, then blue hair and a very downtown kind of look, I chalked up his appearance to youthful rebellion and let it go at that. The kid had major talent, so I didn't care what color his hair was or the fact that he wore skintight leather pants and Lycra tee shirts. His department turned out killer desserts. And P.S., he came to his interview dressed like he was going to church.

For the most part, the best advice is that you channel your creativity and passion into your cooking rather than your appearance. Free spirits, a little wild and crazy, will find it hard making it to the top. They will hit a wall one day—and will not be able to jump it. I am not saying that there is a stereotype for a chef, but cleanliness and neatness reflect pride and respect for this craft.

This need to toe the line in looks and attitude is as it should be, and not just because I am an Old World chef.

You must realize that you are following in the footsteps of two and a half centuries of masters (that is when the world's first true restaurants opened in Paris). Even more, you must realize that you are the transmitter of millennia of food culture and that people come to you with an emotional expectation as well as a culinary one. Your customers trust you to make their birthday, anniversary, first date, engagement, business deal celebration as special as the feelings that go with it. That trust makes you realize fully that haute cuisine is indeed a high calling.

SELF-MANAGEMENT: INTEREST, EGO, FOCUS AND TEAMWORK

Not everything in the career of a chef fits into tidy pigeon-holes. In this letter I would like to offer you a grab bag of qualities, essential but disparate, that I have observed in young cooks who went on to become top-flight chefs in their own right. It all starts with self-management.

For example, some cooks are meticulous in classifying recipes, keeping track of all the details in the kitchen that contribute to a dish. I think such cooks can be very good managers. I remember, in my early days, the chefs who did this were the ones who went on to bigger things. We would get together after work or on days off to compare notes in our diaries and exchange recipes. Remember, back then our mentors (Vergé, Chapel, Haeberlin and so on) did not have their own cookbooks. Often during our afternoon breaks we would trade recipes the way kids trade baseball cards: "Hey, I'll give you three Bocuses for two Haeberlins and a Girardet." You would never get this exchange at the top level—one great chef to another—so this is how valuable "chef DNA" would get mixed, and the result would be ideas for new dishes that were in a sense the offspring of the top chefs of the day.

If you have a deep interest in recipes, it often follows that you understand how to begin to organize the details of a recipe. These are tremendously revealing qualities, because only through understanding the details and organization of a recipe can you achieve consistency, the hallmark of a good kitchen. If I do a terrine of foie gras and there are fifteen cooks and assistants in the kitchen, I look for the person who asks me detailed and insightful questions about the recipe. He or she really wants to understand. The others? They do their job. They may do it well, maybe better than the one who asked the question, but still I think the inquiring chef is the one who, once he or she understands a recipe, will be *consistent*. Remember that word, underline it, put in on your mirror.

People may visit your restaurant once because it sounds interesting. They may visit it a second time because they had a good meal the first time, but they will only keep coming back if you are consistent. The goal of the chef, whatever the level of cuisine, is consistency. Consistency in preparation, technique, taste and presentation—all must come together to meet or exceed the expectations of the guest. The only acceptable departure from the norm is to do it even better than the last time.

This way, people will return to your table just as they might reread *Madame Bovary* or return for a second or third viewing of *The Godfather*; each reexperience reveals new pleasures.

Or, because you are consistent your patrons may trust you to try something completely new. You like my Braised Shortribs? You like my Sea Bass? Then you will probably give me the benefit of the doubt with Skate Wing stuffed with Chanterelles Duxelles on a bed of creamy spinach, glazed with beef bordelaise sauce (which I just happened to have put on the menu as I write this paragraph).

I always look carefully at how a young chef self-manages in the one area where he has some latitude: his production and *mise-en-place* (everything one does before service in order to be ready for service). Say we give you a bunch of leeks to julienne. You are only going to julienne the white parts. The young chef who will improve thinks ahead and asks, "What am I going to do with the greens?" They might be delicious for the staff meal. Or maybe you remember reading about Jean-Georges Vongerichten's lamb saddle dusted with black trumpet mushroom powder and a green leek purée, and you try something in that spirit. If you think like this you have an understanding that in haute cuisine we create a lot of waste, but there is always some way to use almost everything if you think about it long enough.

One of the most memorable dishes I ever made grew out of this natural instinct to use everything and discard nothing, or almost nothing. It was back at the old Daniel on 76th Street in New York. Charlie Trotter and Emeril Lagasse and a half dozen friends came for lunch. Now, one thing you need to know about chefs—we like to cook for each other and we like to raise the bar with something that is really "out there." I had done a suckling pig special two days earlier, so I had two heads sitting in the fridge ready to be given to one of the prep cooks to take home for pozole soup.

Then it occurred to me, why not give these superstar chefs something really primal, like a nice pig's head? I took a large copper sauté pan and meticulously lined it with apple-smoked bacon. Then I put the two heads back to back and surrounded them with rustically cut apples, celery root, carrots, onions, lots of endive, rosemary, garlic, fresh cracked pepper and salt. I pressed the vegetables tight against the pigs' heads then covered the whole thing with slices of bacon so that in effect you had a turban of bacon.

I roasted it for two and a half hours until the bacon was golden and crisp. When we presented the finished dish at the table, we cracked open the bacon crust and the aroma erupted to fill the room with a smoky, unctuous perfume.

I believe Emeril's exact words were, "Yeah, man!"

Then we brought the heads back to the kitchen and gave everybody at Emeril and Charlie's table a piece of ear, snout, brain, some garnish and the smoky *jus*. This is how to make a chef happy when you feed him. Do not give him caviar, give him a pig's head. Needless to say, I do not have much call for bacon-wrapped suckling pig's head. In fact, that was the only time I ever made it. It was an unforgettable, spontaneous moment that I may never recreate, but this is the kind of thing chefs do for one another. Pure whim, going with your gut and having fun.

Which gets me back to my point: *Do not waste anything.* Think instead of how you can fully utilize every ingredient. The young chef who thinks ahead like this has an approach that takes in the total picture, both culinary and financial. Many chefs (including talented home chefs) can create wonderful recipes if they buy expensive ingredients, use them extravagantly and waste all the trimmings and cooking liquids that inevitably are part of any recipe. The true "chef in the raw" instinctively understands that waste brings up food costs, so he or she figures out a way to use the totality of every product. When I see a young chef who thinks this way, it tells me that here is a person who not only understands food, but also understands process and how to organize many things at once.

Do you remember how I told you that you must make yourself valuable to the chef? I am not only giving you good advice, I am doing a favor for whatever chef you work for as you begin your career. You see, everybody thinks that we top chefs are magicians—that we personally have a hand in every dish that comes out of the kitchen. In fact, this is to confuse the orchestra with the conductor.

Of course, a true chef prides himself on his cooking and I pride myself on mine, but the truth is that a chef, as he gets more successful, can no longer cook to the exclusion of everything else. In much the same way, an orchestra conductor may be a wonderful musician, but he spends most of his time leading the band—not playing the piano. So the choice of the personnel with whom we chefs surround ourselves is critical.

If you become a top chef, being good is not good enough. You need to *hire* great. For example, years ago when I was asked to become the chef of the Plaza Athénée in Manhattan, I searched high and low for a great second in command. I heard of a brilliant young Cambodian, Sottha Khun, who was working with Alain Passard just outside Paris. I flew over to have lunch with him and felt that here was a guy who could complement my talents and bring his own special gifts to the table. That meant that I could concentrate on managing and cooking, without imagining that every time I left my station the service would fall apart.

So never worry that someone will come along who is as good as you are. Two good cooks—working as a team—are much more valuable than one good cook. In cooking, as in music, harmony is greater than the sum of its parts. It opens up possibilities that are inaccessible to the solo chef. If you always work with good, dedicated people, both above and below you, then you will learn to thrive in an environment of excellence. At this stage of my career, I would not mind—indeed, I welcome—

people working for me who can cook some things better than I can. Good people raise the whole level of the game. My people are my greatest asset, every one: the pot washer, the pastry cook, the waiters—they are all your allies. Treat them with respect and they will remain an asset. Treat them as interchangeable and expendable and you will have difficulty holding any team together.

It is a fine and delicate balance, dependent on nuance and detail. Take the best team on the road (which often happens when chefs do a guest appearance in another city or country) and the food is rarely as on the money as in that chef's home kitchen. For instance, when, after being in business for five years, I closed the original Daniel on 76th Street (Café Boulud is there now) and moved to 65th Street (ironically, the original home of Le Cirque, where I had cooked for so many years), I took my pots and pans, my recipes and most of my staff and marched them eleven blocks downtown—seemingly not a very big move. But all of those almost instinctual moves in a settled situation—having to reach to the right for a plate rather than the left, the *rôtisserie* station being four steps from the meat line rather than three—affected timing, coordination and inevitably, the end result. We had to relearn to walk, in a way. We were good when we opened the new Daniel, but not as smoothly efficient as when we had left the old Daniel. We were transplanted, and it takes time for any organism to accept a transplant. In the case of a restaurant, it takes time for even the best people to mesh in new surroundings and return to the top of their game.

When you work in a top restaurant, you naturally begin to feel some pride. This is good, but be careful. You need a healthy ego and driving ambition, but you also need to put them on the shelf for a while and concentrate on the needs of the chef for whom you are working. A young chef should give one and a half years of time to his mentor. Out of our hundred cooks, only half will put in a year and a half or more. The rest move every year or so. In my opinion, their ego and ambition get in the way of their progress as a chef.

I know about ego and ambition. I have a healthy dose of both. When I was a cook, I wanted to be a chef de partie. When I was chef de partie, I wanted to be a sous-chef. When I was sous-chef, I wanted to be chef. Then I wanted to be a restaurateur. Then I wanted to open another restaurant. It is inevitable, if you live and breathe this business, that your passion will grow, that this will fuel your ambition and that your ego will help to drive it. These are all good things . . . in good time. But while you are a young chef, the motto in my kitchen is: Leave your jewelry and your ego in the locker room.

▪ PASSING THE WHO CARES TEST

When you become an executive chef, or chef-restaurateur, the first question you must ask yourself every day is, Why would people choose my restaurant? In a great city there are hundreds of choices. As a hip musician friend once asked, "Does it pass the who cares test?" In terms of what's trendy, dozens of restaurants serve diver scallops, free-range beef, line-caught striped bass, lemongrass shrimp, chipotle short ribs. Or more classically, half a dozen places in New York serve as many truffles as we do and have roast squab or the best caviar or any of the de rigueur items at a high-ticket place.

So why would someone pick my place . . . or yours?

At the level of restaurant we are talking about, food is the first consideration, although comfort level (both emotional and physical) in the dining room also comes into play. That you have technique is taken for granted. That you can afford the best and most expensive ingredients is also a foregone conclusion. It is not about price. Nor, surprisingly, is it about perfection.

Perfection can be boring. If you caught big fish every time you went fishing, if your team won every time you turned on the television, where's the thrill, the surprise, the joy? A perfectly roasted chicken tastes the same at my restaurant, at Laurent Manrique's Aqua in San Francisco, at Flora Mikula's in Paris. What makes each different is what makes one painter or one author different from another . . . the soul of the artist.

I do not mean this in some New Age sense (although a succulent leg of spring lamb can transport me into mystical ecstasy). I mean it in the direct sense that the food has to give you a feeling of well-being. It needs to make you happy. Yes, the technique must be perfect, meticulous and precise. Yes, it must amaze you. But first and last it must make you happy.

There are chefs who accomplish this through a daring and complex combination of ingredients and techniques. I mentioned Gray Kunz of Lespinasse and his balance of the Indian, French and Chinese palates, or the wonderful Ferran Adria at El Bulli in Spain or Pierre Gagniere in Paris—but they are exceptions. Complexity is rewarding and even remarkable, but when the result, as in many cases, is simply a fusillade of culinary fireworks, it can leave you amazed but not touched. As a chef, you want to move your patrons, touch them, reawaken their fantasies of travel, their memories of childhood; they want to trust you to take them on a culinary voyage where your imagination is their guiding star (and when it is all done, they make a reservation for their next visit as they leave).

It all comes down to balance on the part of the chef. I constantly think of the creative tension between eccentricity and simplicity. The former without the latter leads to a grand fireworks display, but no oomph. Light but no heat. That is why I think simplicity is so important.

Jean and Pierre Troisgros put it very wisely when I was a young chef. They spoke of *La Règle de Trois*, or The Rule of Three. By this they meant that there should be three main components in a dish. For example, they did salmon, white wine sauce and sorrel. A strong oceanic flavor tempered by the smooth creaminess of the wine sauce and the tanginess of the sorrel. Another inspiration, purely Lyonnais, is the combination of frog legs in a watercress velouté alongside crayfish and wild mushrooms that the chef at DB Bistro Moderne, Jean François Bruel, dreamed up. Three traditional ingredients from my home region (Bocuse's and Jean François's as well) served in a new way. Eccentric? Yes. Simple? Yes. But also inspired, which is why it has become a classic that has endured for thirty years.

Or take one of my signature dishes, the paupiette of sea bass. I have probably sold more orders of this in my career than anything else. It's very simple: sea bass in a crust of thin potato slices, served on a bed of leeks with a pungent, highly concentrated red wine sauce. I think part of the reason this became a classic in my repertoire, of course, has to do with its pleasing combination of tastes and textures, but equally so, its simplicity makes it something that will linger in your taste memory.

I am reminded of a meal that I had when I took my *sommelier*, Jean Luc Le Dû, to France to spend time with some of the great winemakers of Burgundy and the Rhône valley. It was a real party. Me, Jean Luc, Tom Danziger (my lawyer), my good friend Dean Santon, and Peter Kaminsky, who was writing about my new restaurant for *New York* magazine. Dean, the master of mix tapes, made us an entire trip's worth of traveling music: Howlin' Wolf, Django Reinhardt, The Clash, Bob Dylan. We had a big black BMW. I called this journey The 100,000 Calorie Tour because we ate more great food more often than you would think possible. In fact, some of the guys were convinced it was impossible, but when amazing food is on the agenda, somehow my capacity is hardly ever reached. As for wine, some days the tastings went from nine in the morning to seven at night. Even if you just look at that many wine bottles in a day, it kind of goes to your head.

Making our way slowly to Burgundy, we stopped off at Georges Blanc in Vonnas. The place had grown since I worked there nearly thirty years ago. Such an elegant but unfussy establishment. The wine room in the back of the restaurant was beautifully lit and, just to separate the true gourmets from casual foodies, Georges had one small shelf filled with bottles of *eau de vipère*—a French farmhouse tradition. Whenever a poisonous snake is found in a barn or around the house, farm families (including mine) would capture the snake, stick it in a wine bottle, fill the bottle with *eau de vie* and let it sit for a few years. Because of the curve of the bottle, which acts like a big magnifying glass, you see this giant snake head.

Georges had about twenty well-pickled vipers lined up on that shelf and it always got *ooh la la*'s, especially from the ladies and children. Georges made us a lovely tasting menu and months later, when someone asked me to name the most memorable dish that we had on our trip, it was not the amazing turbot en croûte from l'Espérance nor the rich and bold veal en cocotte with carrots and orange juice from Bernard Louiseau at La Côte d'Or nor the equally dazzling partridge and porcinis at Lameloise. What I remembered most was an exceedingly simple Georges Blanc vichyssoise with scallops, oysters and caviar—in other words, a basic peasant dish, vichyssoise, transformed by additional ingredients into something noble and sublime. Simplicity and eccentricity made it memorable. Or to cite another example, our executive chef at Daniel, Alex Lee, drew on his Asian heritage and sense of spices and herbs to create an unforgettable ginger-crusted lobster with a peashoot emulsion and spiced carrot purée.

Eccentric, yes, but not so eccentric that it leaves people scratching their heads. Remember, if you are successful in establishing an identity, people will have certain expectations of you. If you have concentrated on a certain culinary tradition, then your eccentric dishes cannot be terribly far afield.

Cities such as Paris, London, New York and San Francisco have a tremendous variety of national styles in their restaurants, so you can afford to be more venturesome there than in some other towns. In Alsace, for example, while there are wonderful *weinstubes* (local cafés that serve traditional *tarte flambée* and *choucroute*) or gastronomic temples such as Le Crocodile in Strasbourg, there is very little cuisine outside of this local tradition. To my way of thinking, staying in the provinces leaves out a lot of the fun of discovery one finds in multiethnic metropolises. Still, you are who you are, and the further you go in this business, the more your clientele will expect specific focus in your cuisine.

This is why I advise you once again to look to a culinary tradition that makes both you and your clientele comfortable. For me, French cuisine has the longevity and depth to make it a resource of tradition as well as a source of inspiration and creativity. Italian cuisine fits this bill too. Less predictably (if all you know of Mexican food are burritos and tacos), Rick Bayless at Topalabompo in Chicago has embraced the cuisines of Mexico and created what many consider to be the world's greatest Mexican restaurant, in or out of Mexico.

In New York, Floyd Cardoz has combined French technique and Indian ingredients at Tabla. Doug Rodriguez, the Cuban American wonder boy, has somehow managed to assimilate Caribbean, Peruvian and Ecuadorian traditions into an authentic Latin statement that has come to be known as Nueva Latina. In all of these cases, you will note that the chef's innovations remain within a tradition. I personally feel you are most secure within the European tradition, but if you choose some other cuisine, first make sure that it awakes a passion in you, second, that you know it well, and equally important, make sure that there is a market for it.

The thing that you want to avoid above all is a crazy eclecticism. Or as my old boss at Le Cirque, Sirio Maccioni, put it with savvy directness, "Fusion, okay, Confusion, not okay!"

So you walk this line between innovation and tradition. You need the innovation, the eccentricity, to keep yourself interested and engaged. That is how I came up with a dish that I would call eccentric but also simple and direct. Like many modern chefs, I love sushi. In fact, late at night I used to love nothing more than showing up with a bunch of chefs around midnight at Sushihatsu on the East Side. Nothing about it made you think it was special. No high concept design. No limos. No slinky models. Just a simple wooden sushi bar that looked like every other sushi bar in every city in America.

But inside, oh, what great ingredients at a convenient place that was open until 3 A.M.! Beautiful Japanese mackerel. *Toro* as tender and pink as milk-fed veal. Hand rolls with crisp salmon skin and *uni*. I rarely got out of there for less than $150. I would eat for hours, and I would not be filled.

After years of eating there, I traveled in South America where I became more familiar with ceviche. Given my love of these two uncooked fish "cuisines," I felt confident that I could try something in the raw seafood vein that would be true to my "inner chef." The result—part Daniel, part Georges Blanc, part Japanese, part Peruvian—was an oyster filled with slices of scallops and caviar, Chincoteague oysters, a sprinkle of lime, oyster liquor, grated horseradish and a garnish of crunchy celery, radishes, minced chives and a dab of *uni*. A simple dish, all about balance and composition, but mostly it is about the purity and freshness of the sea, slightly briny with notes of the aromatic sharpness of iodine. Key to the concept of this dish is that the ingredients are so fresh, there is a delicate, almost fragile quality to the completed recipe.

Where did that dish come from? From a growing acquaintance with sushi, from the oysters of my childhood, from the ceviche bars of Lima and from a certain hunger that goes off in a chef when you have assimilated tastes and techniques to the extent that a dish—or at least the idea for it—comes to you the way that daydreams do. All of a sudden, it is just there.

Creativity and innovation are forced upon you if you have a market-driven menu meeting the expectations of a knowledgeable and novelty-seeking clientele. When you are in tune with the markets, you will come up with specials every day. For as long as I have been in the kitchen, that has been one of the most exciting aspects of the job, a daily dose of unfettered freedom.

It is also where the whole team comes into play. As a chef, you must have the confidence in yourself and your team that allows you to be open to the ideas of the cooks. Believe me, they are full of ideas and grateful for the chance to express them. The daily special may come from one of them or may start with one person's idea and bounce around the kitchen until finally there is something worthy of your dining room.

Go with the flow. Also go slow. New dishes evolve and gain complexity as they do. They also need new techniques, or at least new combinations of techniques, and most of all, their own unique balance of tastes. I do not have all the answers in my repertoire. We learn as a group. True, I give direction, but my chef de cuisine or sous-chef will have the main task of working it out and may know something new about an ingredient or a method that we will all share. The great lesson in all this is that cuisine is not written in stone. It evolves every day.

There is a difference between creating a recipe and creating a painting. If an artist feels that he is losing it at the easel, he can get up, take a rest, leave it for another day. Once you start cooking something, though, you cannot uncook it; you have to keep going until you finish. The result may not always be right for the menu, but you should see things through to the end so that you can at least pick out a few successful elements and apply them in the future.

You may not be the one who makes the correction that completes a dish. You may take it 90 percent of the way, but then someone will add 5 percent and someone else will add 2 percent or 3 percent until an almost good enough dish becomes something new and exciting. Feedback from the front-of-the-house is also always helpful. Finally, when you have a new recipe exactly how you want it, then you do write it in stone. Turn your creativity to the next new dish.

Innovation and creation are what keep this job interesting. Of course, you must know how to make a perfect *coq au vin*, but if all you do is turn out culinary Xeroxes of the classic dishes, in time you will become bored and even the classics will lose some of their gusto. Failed recipes are never the problem. Failing to try to create them is.

THE FRONT
OF THE HOUSE

You may become a marvelous chef, the inventor of a whole new cuisine. You may have *Food & Wine* absolutely gaga over your recipes—but if the people in your restaurant who interact with the public are not on their game, it really does not matter. Your customers only *think* that they come to a restaurant merely for the food. What they really come for is more complex than that. Sure they want a good meal, but they also want a pleasant time, nice surroundings and a staff that treats them as if service is a pleasure.

A great front of the house with so-so food is liable to be more successful than a restaurant with mind-blowing food and surly waiters and maitre d's. Everyone pays lip service to great service, but in the day-to-day crush of getting the meals cooked and served, it is easy to lose sight of what is going on outside the kitchen, beyond those double doors, where the check gets paid.

Do not ever lose sight of this. Every time you do, it will come back to bite you. If you really want to learn what service is all about, the best teacher—as in everything—is experience. When I was an apprentice in the kitchen in Lyon, I worked at the brasserie next door (on my day off). They were short one waiter, so I offered to help the owner. I figured the owner could use the extra hand, and by the same token, I knew I could stand to learn a bit more about service. There was then (and to some extent, still is) a natural tension between wait staff and kitchen staff. The front of the house is thought of as more white collar, with a tendency to put on airs. The kitchen, though more blue collar, is also felt to be more artistic (at least by those of us who work in the back).

I quickly came to appreciate the mix of personality traits that go into the makeup of a good waiter: In a fine dining restaurant you need to be intelligent, often multilingual, confident and yet at the same time, humble. I may have been smart for a young cook, but I was not a very good waiter. Still, I had a valuable experience. Up close and firsthand I saw that there are customers who are in a hurry, customers who change their mind, customers who "distinctly remember" asking for something other than what you serve them. There are chatty people, courteous people and people who would not be pleased if Escoffier himself cooked the meal and served it on Napoleon's personal plates.

The front of the house has to deal with all of these types and, though it is a test of your composure, you must treat each of them with the same care. That is what being a professional means. Being courteous to a charming customer is easy; being nice to a pain in the neck is professional.

In America, French restaurants with French staff have a reputation for being haughty or difficult. I am reminded of a cartoon that I once saw in *National Lampoon*. A snooty waiter, with a pencil-thin moustache, looks on with disdain at a horrified couple. In front of them is a tray with something burned to a cinder, and still smoking. "It is a burnt telephone book," the waiter explains. "We gave it a fancy French name and you ordered it." Although this is extreme, I have heard of naïve customers going into a Paris bistro and ordering *andouillette* because it sounds like *andouille* (a Cajun specialty), then being traumatized when a bundle of calf intestines coated with mustard arrives.

I think it is unfortunate that French restaurants have a reputation for inaccessibility, one that they do not deserve. True, there are haughty waiters and captains (I fire them pretty quickly), but I think some of this antipathy can be explained by the fact that many people do not speak French and feel insecure with all those French words, fancy European manners, massive wine lists, and a wine steward with an ego to match.

The job of the restaurateur is to overcome this feeling and make people feel comfortable in any language. In some cases, the inherent personal dynamics of the restaurant as a scene of social interaction work decidedly against you. I am thinking in particular of the customer who has a chip on his or her shoulder no matter what you do. Your being nice may not change things very much. Part of the explanation for the natural combativeness of some diners is that we live in a world where we all have to take orders and swallow our pride while some overbearing blowhard tears us apart. The client-restaurant relationship is one of the few opportunities the customer has to be in a position of superiority: Bad day at the office? Got blamed for something you didn't do? Belittled for a shortcoming? You can always take it out on the waiter.

That the wait staff has done nothing or very little to deserve this is beside the point. The customer lets it out simply because he or she can. It is human nature. The anger has to go somewhere, and not getting the order exactly right or exactly on time is reason enough to dredge up the day's stored resentments. Furthermore, the bigger your reputation as a restaurateur, the more people will feel entitled to have things exactly their way and to let you know when they are not.

Do not take this personally but rather as a challenge. Remember, in this business we use one word for the whole ensemble of activities, from cloakroom to kitchen to the dining room, that make up the restaurant experience. That word is *service*. Your job is to serve, politely, professionally and sincerely. The little things that make people feel special—from a smile at the door to a well-considered wine recommendation—can mean so much. Bear in mind that in a well-run restaurant, the unhappy and unsatisfiable represent a very small percentage; still, if not dealt with, they can ruin the night for you and your staff.

When you make steady customers out of perennial complainers, you can take some pride in knowing that their business is "found money" for you.

Never, ever argue with a customer. Never allow your staff to do so either. I had a maitre d' working for me at a time when I thought I might be able to combine two jobs in the interest of economy. This guy had very good references and had worked in some terrific New York restaurants. He also had miles of attitude. One day I saw him arguing with a customer. About forty-five seconds later he became my former maitre d'.

Complaints, by the way, are not always unfounded. They are right as often as they are wrong and they are invaluable. When you have a famous restaurant, almost everyone will tell you how great your food is and how great your place is. That is nice, but it does not necessarily help you improve.

Criticism, on the other hand, helps you make corrections. Teach your staff to be attentive to criticism. Some customers will be very direct when they are not happy and let you know it. Others may feel unsure or at least uncomfortable in voicing displeasure, but they too communicate through body language and loss of enthusiasm. The staff must have their antennae up. Often they can sense dissatisfaction in the dining room and address it before it gets to you.

For example, while some diners come for a transcendental once-in-a-lifetime experience, some of our most loyal regulars come just as much for consistency and familiarity. Our wait staff quickly learn that these diners do not want to be dazzled by some new invention every night. They want a cocktail, good wine and their favorite food. The challenge is to lead these diners past their old favorites to the occasional new recipe. This can be a help to the kitchen because these members of the "dining family" often will be more frank in helping critique a new dish.

You might also consider doing as we do and hire completely anonymous reviewers to come to your restaurant icognito and deliver a thorough eight-page critique of a typical three-hour dining experience: from making the reservation, to how long it took to get a martini, to the attentiveness of the wait staff, and, of course, to the cuisine. It is money well spent.

Problems, though, are unavoidable. Frequently, a situation can start in the lounge with a delay in seating (more than half an hour becomes a serious concern). A free round of drinks and some canapés go a long way toward pacifying restless patrons. Just as important, the waiter in the dining room needs to know that the customer has been made to wait, and he or she should make the kitchen aware of the need to be super prompt. When we have unhappy or potentially unhappy customers, the staff is authorized to give them an extra appetizer or dessert "with the special compliments of the chef." The small incremental food cost is negligible compared to the cost of losing potential business.

If, as sometimes happens, we get a letter of complaint, we know who the waiter was, who the assistant was and what was ordered. We figure out what went wrong and how to avoid the same mistake happening again. In this we are helped by our logbook in which each night every head of department records what happened, good and bad. From a waiter's having run too fast in the dining room to the bread boy cutting the bread too thickly to a customer expressing dissatisfaction with a wine. The plusses and minuses in that logbook become the agenda for the next day's preservice meeting where we revisit every issue.

The log and the preservice meeting also assist in knowing when to make extra-special nice to an unhappy customer. You have no idea how much a personal call or letter from the chef will do in terms of good will.

Sometimes a problem is nobody's fault. It is just the nature of the business, because you cannot know in advance how the evening is going to play out. People arrive late. They cancel. Their reservation for seven becomes a reservation for three (and vice versa). Feeding a hundred and fifty people in a restaurant over the course of an evening is different than entertaining a hundred and fifty people in a theater.

In the theater, the performance goes on whether twenty people show up, two hundred and twenty, or a full house. In a restaurant, the "performance" is constantly in flux and the whole evening is a series of separate performances, in a manner of speaking: each diner reacting to the particular way he or she is treated and whether the chef meets, exceeds or falls short of expectations. The only thing you can be sure of is that a lot of curve balls will be thrown at you and you just deal with them until the evening is through.

If you are owner and chef, as I am, you may very well find yourself making the rounds in the dining room a few times during service. I think this is a great idea, but it is not for every chef. Joel Robuchon, for example, rarely came out, but he was acknowledged to be the top chef in Paris.

I got into the habit of visiting the dining room at Le Cirque, when I would occasionally go out to take special orders or, as time went by, just to take the temperature of the room. By now these visits are second nature to me. I try to pick a time when the pressure is not at its peak in the kitchen—say, in between seatings or at the beginning or end of service.

I do not necessarily speak with everybody in the dining room. Some people prefer not to be disturbed, but a great many enjoy the sense of being hosted when the chef stops by. You will know, from eye contact or body language, if your presence will be welcome. If it is, give each conversation your full attention. Do not be looking around the room to see if someone more famous or powerful is acting fidgety. If you make contact with a customer, train yourself to focus on him or her for the few minutes you are with that person.

Sometimes, when things are busy and the wait staff is backed up, I will take an order or help serve something tableside. The staff appreciates it. The customers appreciate it. And it actually helps in a practical sense.

Bottom line: Do whatever it takes to make things go smoothly and everybody stays happy. You will be greatly assisted if you have at least one talented shmoozer in the dining room management, someone skilled in making people feel at ease (it goes without saying that the rest of the wait staff must be eager to please as well). The style of this shmoozer is important. Make sure he or she reflects who you are. Attentiveness and courtesy work better for me than boisterous glad-handing.

Having said that you must treat everyone courteously and warmly, it is human nature to take a little extra care with your best customers. After all, they have made the investment in you. Recently, I had a customer who had spent thousands of dollars on wine with us. At the end of one of my tasting menus he said, "Wonderful, exquisite, but I would love some tripe."

So the next week, when he came back, I put tripe on the menu, a very basic peasant dish, but dolled up with chorizo, black olives, cranberry beans, calf's feet, tomato confit and a buttery crust of sourdough bread. Yes I cooked to order, in a sense, but I did it in my very own way. So although I will listen to my customers, try to meet their requests, I assume that when they ask me for something special they want my style. It is the same in every great or even good restaurant.

IS THERE LIFE
AFTER RESTAURANTS?

One thing that becomes apparent to you very quickly is that when the rest of the world is having fun, you are working. Saturday night, you work; Christmas, you work; Easter, Fourth of July, Mother's Day, Thanksgiving . . . ditto. If you want to be a chef, you cannot compare your life to others. The chef's world is a different world. The hours are longer, the work more intense than in many other walks of life. But you really do not dwell on it, at least I don't.

Sure I would love to go to more movies, go out with my friends more, spend more time at home, but I made a choice when I was fourteen and I never looked back. Restaurants are my passion and they consume me. If anything, as time goes by, restaurant life becomes more consuming. As perfection becomes more attainable, it also becomes more and more the center of your life. Where other passions may cool with time, the chef's gets hotter.

Anyone who can find this kind of guiding passion in life is very lucky, because so many people never experience the sense of mission and maturing skill that a chef's career brings. From your first day, you must seek out the best mentors, the best restaurants, the best suppliers and the best partners as you go through this career, because you are only as good as the background you acquire and the people with whom you work.

I do not mean to suggest that being a chef requires self-denial, like some medieval monk. The restaurant kitchen—sensual, raucous and intense—becomes its own world. You may not get to hang out with friends that much outside of work, but you will develop deep friendships in the kitchen. And you will be doing the thing you love the most.

In the end, doing what you love is what matters and will make you a better chef. The sacrifices, even the successes, are add-ons. The heart of the matter is that you are doing what you love. As time passes, your ambition will carry you from one milestone to another: from mastering a recipe to opening your own restaurant. The further you go, the more you will be controlled by your passion and ambition to become bigger, to open more places, to do more. At a certain point, achieving success is no longer a distant goal. At that point, taking control of your success and balancing it with being a parent, spouse and friend takes center stage.

As it is with a good recipe, combining these ingredients for living can be endlessly fine-tuned, reworked, reinvented; for each of us, something different. As for working out that recipe . . . well, I cannot tell you the measurements, but I hope I have been able to get you started.

Now go cook! And maybe one day I will be reading your book.

■ THE TEN COMMANDMENTS OF A CHEF

1. Keep Your Knives Sharp

Your most basic tool is your knife. To cut well all of your knives must be sharp. Make sharpening a daily ritual at the very least. A knife is not like a car that breaks down. If it does not perform, you have not kept it sharp. Remember, it is never the knife's fault.

2. Work with the Best People

To become a great chef you do not need to work with twenty top chefs. You need to experience three or four very good chefs. The best is not necessarily the most popular or most famous, it can just as easily be a chef in a small place who is simply very organized and very good. Focus on a few chefs for your foundation, then for specialties—for example, charcuterie, pastry and so on—you can do internships.

3. Keep Your Station Orderly

From the storage of vegetables to the finishing of *mise-en-place*, everything needs to be marked, labeled and in the proper containers, taking up the minimum of room. Then, during service, you will not be in the weeds. Instead, you will be able to fill orders with maximum efficiency. A well-organized station also gets respect from the rest of the kitchen.

4. Purchase Wisely

The profitable restaurant runs on the same principle as the frugal housewife's kitchen: Use everything, because everything you do not use is potential profit that goes straight into the garbage. Any underutilized food item will affect your food costs. Pay attention to the price of ingredients and keep them in line with what a customer will pay for a dish. The more you utilize everything, the more you will be able to afford the best ingredients. A great chef respects the culinary value of every ingredient—from truffle to turnip.

5. Season with Precision

The taste of every ingredient is elevated by proper seasoning. There is an exact point at which ingredients are seasoned correctly. More is not always better. Learning the peculiarities of your palate and attuning it to finished results requires precision and endless practice.

6. Master the Heat

From 120°F to 800°F—there is an enormous range for heat to affect ingredients. A truly great cook has such an intimate knowledge of heat that he or she develops a sixth sense of timing for the moment of doneness. Learn the basics of heat so that you can cook easily with every form of heat in the classical repertoire.

7. Learn the World of Food

Experience different cuisines whenever you can. Do it when you are young, before you are building your career. Learning other cuisines will broaden your foundation as a chef. Even when you have begun to progress through the ranks of the kitchen, use your time off to go places, try new restaurants, buy books. In other words, immerse yourself in the world of food.

8. Know the Classics

No matter what cuisine you concentrate on, the classic dishes will cover the spectrum of techniques and ingredients needed to master a cuisine. The fundamentals of stocks, sauces and seasoning are all there in the classics . . . whether that classic is clam chowder in Cape Cod or bouillabaisse in Marseilles.

9. Accept Criticism

As a young chef, you spend your days and nights being criticized and analyzed by the chefs for whom you work. It is important to learn from criticism. It is equally important to learn how to criticize usefully when you become a full-fledged chef. And finally, you must learn from the criticism of the public. Recognize that to keep yourself interested you are constantly varying, innovating and reinventing, succeeding at times and needing more work at others. Criticism is the public's way of telling you how to improve on the results of your creative impulses.

10. Keep a Journal of Your Recipes

You cannot remember everything you see cooked, or even have cooked, but with a journal, a computer, a digital camera, you can bring those taste memories to life . . . to guide you for the rest of your professional life.

■ "You Are What You Have Cooked": A Selection of Favorite Recipes

There is an expression in English: "you are what you eat." For a chef it would be closer to the truth to say "you are what you have cooked." From the first time I scrambled an egg in my parents' kitchen, to the many times I have cooked something new and elaborate for a president or a movie star, my autobiography is really a collection of the food I have made. I thought it would be unfair in a book that describes food with such passion, for me to leave you hungry for more. So from every place that I have lived and cooked here are some recipes and inspirations that I can truly say I love the most.

Chicken Grand-Mère Francine

Everybody's grandmother makes a chicken fricassée, and my grandmother, Francine, was no exception. She was a sweet lady and cooked at our original family restaurant, Café Boulud. Until she was seven years old she didn't speak French, but, rather, the ancient language of my region Dauphinois. Mastering this dish means you have learned how to caramelize meat properly, one of the most important techniques for any chef—in the restaurant or at home.

MAKES 4 SERVINGS

2 tablespoons extra-virgin olive oil

One 3-pound chicken, cut into 8 pieces

Salt and freshly ground white pepper

2 tablespoons unsalted butter

12 cipollini onions, peeled and trimmed

4 shallots, peeled and trimmed

2 heads garlic, cloves separated but not peeled

3 sprigs thyme

4 small Yukon gold potatoes, peeled and cut into
 $1^1/_2$-inch chunks

2 small celery roots, peeled and cut into $1^1/_2$ inch
 chunks

2 ounces slab bacon, cut into short, thin strips

12 small cremini or oyster mushrooms, cleaned and
   trimmed

2 cups unsalted chicken stock or low-sodium chicken
   broth

1. Center a rack in the oven and preheat the oven to
375°F.

2. Working over medium-high heat, warm the olive
oil in a 12-inch ovenproof sauté pan or skillet—choose
one with high sides and a cover. Season the chicken
pieces all over with salt and pepper, slip them into the
pan, and cook until they are well browned on all sides,
about 10 to 15 minutes. Take your time—you want a
nice, deep color, and you also want to cook the chickens
three-quarters through at this point. When the chicken
is deeply golden, transfer it to a platter and keep it in a
warm place while you work on the vegetables.

3. Pour off all but 2 tablespoons of the cooking fat
from the pan. Lower the heat to medium, add the butter,
the onions, shallots, garlic and thyme and cook and stir
just until the vegetables start to take on a little color,
about 3 minutes. Add the potatoes, celery root, and bacon and cook 1 to 2 minutes, just to start rendering the
bacon fat. Cover the pan and cook another 10 minutes,
stirring every 2 minutes.

4. Add the mushrooms, season with salt and pepper and return the chicken to the pan. Add the chicken stock, bring to the boil, and slide the pan into the oven. Bake, uncovered, for 20 to 25 minutes, or until the chicken is cooked through. Spoon everything onto a warm serving platter or into an attractive casserole.

To serve: Bring the chicken to the table, with plenty of pieces of crusty baguette to sop up the sauce and spread with the soft, caramely garlic that is easily squeezed out of its skin.

Originally appeared in the *Café Boulud Cookbook*, by Daniel Boulud and Dorie Greenspan (Scribner, 1999).

■ ■ ■

Daniel Boulud

St. Pierre de Chandieu — The '60s

Lamb Barboton

In the winter time, it was often quite wet and raw at our farm. You needed something to warm up your insides and "stick to your ribs," as they say in America. I always think of my mother making this for Sunday lunch, kind of an Irish stew done Lyonnais style, with the fragrance of serpolet, our Provençal wild thyme. My mother would usually serve it with creamed spinach.

MAKES 4 TO 6 SERVINGS

3 pounds boneless lamb shoulder, trimmed of fat and
    cut into 2-inch chunks
All-purpose flour
Salt and freshly ground black pepper
4 tablespoons unsalted butter
2 large onions (approximately 1 pound), peeled and
    cut into ½-inch wedges
2 medium leeks (approximately ¼ pound), white and
    light green parts only, thoroughly washed, and cut
    into ½-inch segments
2 cloves garlic, finely chopped
1 cup dry white wine, preferably a Chardonnay
3 pounds Yukon Gold or other yellow-fleshed
    potatoes, peeled and quartered or cut into 1½-inch
    cubes, and reserved in cold water

6 to 8 cups unsalted chicken stock or low-sodium
chicken broth

2 sprigs thyme, preferably wild (*serpolet*)

2 sprigs winter savory

1 bay leaf

2 sprigs flat-leaf parsley, leaves only, minced

1. Center a rack in the oven and preheat the oven to
350°F.

2. Lightly dust the lamb with the flour and season
with salt and pepper. In an enameled cast-iron Dutch
oven or any thick-sided oven-proof roasting dish, warm
2 tablespoons butter over medium-high heat. Add the
lamb and brown on all sides, 6 to 10 minutes. Add
the remaining butter, onions, leek and garlic and sweat
the vegetables, without color, until translucent, 8 to 10
minutes. Add the wine and let the liquid reduce by
three-quarters. Add the potatoes and stock, making sure
that the lamb and vegetables are covered by 1½ to 2
inches of liquid. Add the thyme, savory and bay leaf and
mix well to incorporate. Cover the pan loosely with a lid
or with an oiled or buttered parchment paper pricked
with a tiny air hole in the center. Bring back to a boil and
transfer the pot to the pre-heated oven.

3. Bake the stew for 1½ to 2 hours. The lamb should
be very tender and the potatoes should be soft and begin
to break, so that they thicken the sauce. Cook a half hour

longer, if necessary. Discard the parchment, if using, the thyme, savory and bay leaf.

4. Ladle the stew into shallow rim soup bowls and sprinkle with parsley just before serving. Serve with freshly ground pepper and *fleur de sel* on the side.

Originally appeared in *The Pleasures of Slow Food: Celebrating Authentic Traditions, Flavors, and Recipes,* by Corby Kummer (Chronical Books, 2002).

■　■　■

Lyon (the capital of saucisson) — 1969

Cervelas Sausage with Pistachios

When I first went to work in Lyon, I lived with my uncle who was a charcutier. On my day off I would help him out, especially when things got crazy busy in the holiday season. This pistachio sausage was very much in demand that time of year, I kind of think of it as the most extravagant of poached saucisson, especially when you throw in some truffles. They're expensive, I know, but for Christmas, you might not feel too bad about splurging.

MAKES SIX TO SEVEN 6-INCH SAUSAGES

1 pound 6 ounces pork shoulder (or pork cheek
   meat), cut into 1-inch chunks, well chilled
14 ounces fat back, cut into 1-inch chunks, well
   chilled
4 teaspoons fine sea salt, plus additional
1 teaspoon freshly ground black pepper, plus
   additional
Pinch of cayenne pepper
Pinch of sugar
1 tablespoon Calvados, cognac or brandy
4 to 5 feet calf sausage casing, about 1½ to 2 inches
   in diameter
½ cup shelled pistachio nuts
2 pounds fingerling potatoes, scrubbed

4 tablespoons unsalted butter

1 tablespoon finely chopped flat-leaf parsley

1. Pass the pork shoulder and fat back through a meat grinder set on the largest holes. Transfer the ground meat to a bowl and add the salt, black pepper, cayenne, sugar and Calvados. Mix well, cover with plastic wrap and refrigerate until needed.

2. Set up the sausage stuffer. Rinse the casings thoroughly, both inside and out, under cold running water. Drain well and slide nearly the entire length of the casing onto the funnel feeder, scrunching it up as you go. Tie a knot at the free end and keep it close to the tip of the funnel feeder.

3. Remove the meat from the refrigerator and mix in the pistachio nuts. Turn the machine on and slowly add some of the stuffing, gently holding and guiding the casing with your free hand so that it fills evenly and firmly. Stuff a 6 inch link, being careful to avoid air bubbles, and then leave a 1/4 inch bit of empty casing before making a second link. Repeat with the remaining stuffing and then detach from the machine. Twist the casing at the empty spots or tie with kitchen string to form distinct and separate links. Tie the ends closed and cut off any remaining excess casing. Let rest uncovered in the refrigerator for at least 2 days and up to 4 days to allow the casing to dry out a bit as well as to let the meat rest.

4. Using a small needle, prick the sausages a few times per link. Put them in a pot along with the potatoes and add enough cold water to cover at least 1 to 2 inches. Bring to a boil, lower the heat and simmer very gently until the potatoes are tender enough to be pierced with a fork or the point of a knife, 15 to 20 minutes. Reserve warm in the liquid until serving.

To serve: Drain the sausages and potatoes and cut the sausages into separate links. Season the potatoes with salt and pepper, toss them with the butter and parsley, and place them in the center of a warm serving platter. Arrange the sausages on top and serve immediately.

■ ■ ■

Ascain — 1971

Trout à la Crème with Chorizo and Peppers

When I took my first trip away from my home region, it was to work in the Pay Basque at a place that only had a coal stove. The mountains were full of rivers. The rivers were full of trout. And at the Hotel Etchola in Ascain, the cellar was full of aging Bayonne hams. Sometimes we would get so busy and the orders came so fast and furiously that we would throw four or five trout in a pan, and poach them with cream and vegetables and send them out to the dining room full of folks on holiday.

MAKES 4 SERVINGS

1 green bell pepper, cored, seeded, and deveined
1 red bell pepper, cored, seeded, and deveined
1 yellow bell pepper, cored, seeded, and deveined
1 small onion
1 medium tomato, peeled and seeded
4 ounces chorizo
2 cups heavy cream
$^1/_2$ teaspoon piment d'Espelette (Espelette pepper)
Four 6- to 8-ounce trout, cleaned and boned
Salt and freshly ground white pepper
8 to 12 slices unsmoked, cured dry ham, such as
    Jambon de Bayonne, Serrano ham, or prosciutto

1. Center a rack in the oven and preheat the oven to 350°F.

2. Cut the green, red, and yellow bell peppers, onion, tomato and chorizo into 1- by ¼-inch-thick strips.

3. In an oval fish pan or a 12-inch ovenproof skillet, mix together the peppers, onion, tomato, chorizo, cream and piment d'Espelette and bring to a boil. Reduce the heat to a low simmer and cook until the cream has reduced and thickened, 35 to 40 minutes.

4. Meanwhile, season the inside of each trout with salt and pepper. On a flat work surface, lay 2 to 3 ham slices vertically, slightly overlapping each other. Place the trout across the center of the ham slices. One by one, wrap each piece of ham around the trout. Continue until all four trout are wrapped. Add the fish to the pan and bake for 30 minutes until the fish are cooked through. Serve immediately.

■ ■ ■

Daniel Boulud

Vonnas — 1973

Crêpes Vonnassiennes

When I arrived at La Mère Blanc, it was the first time I worked with women in the kitchen. Georges Blanc's mother was still there on weekends, and there were also two women in the kitchen whose only job was to oversee some of the traditional dishes: Frog's Legs, Poulet à la Crème, and Crêpes Vonassiennes. Truly nobody could approach the super touch that Marie, one of the women chefs, had with this dish. She had a magic touch.

MAKES ABOUT 4 DOZEN CRÊPES

1 pound Yukon Gold or Idaho potatoes, peeled and
   roughly chopped
3 tablespoons milk
3 tablespoons all-purpose flour
3 large eggs
4 large egg whites
2 tablespoons crème fraîche
Salt and freshly ground white pepper
Clarified butter

1. Put the potatoes in a large pot of salted cold water, bring to the boil, and cook until the potatoes are tender enough to be pierced with a fork or the point of a knife, about 15 minutes. Drain the potatoes and return them to

the pot. Set the pot over medium heat and, shaking the pot to keep the potatoes from sticking, cook just until the potatoes are dry, 1 to 2 minutes. Pull the pot from the heat and spoon the potatoes into a food mill fitted with the fine blade or a potato ricer. Push the potatoes through the food mill or ricer into a large bowl. Stir in the milk and let the potatoes cool to room temperature. Using a whisk, stir in the flour, eggs, egg whites and crème fraîche, mixing well after each addition. The mixture should have the consistency of a thick custard. Season to taste with salt and pepper.

2. Warm 1 tablespoon butter in a large non-stick skillet over high heat. When the butter is hot, spoon as many 2-inch circles of batter as will fit in the pan. Cook until golden brown, 20 to 30 seconds. Flip the crêpes over and cook on the second side until golden brown, 20 to 30 seconds. Repeat with the remaining batter, adding butter to the pan as needed. Transfer the crêpes to a paper towel-lined plate. Serve warm either as a side dish or sprinkle with confectioner's sugar and serve as a dessert.

With thanks to Georges Blanc and *Larousse Gastronomique*.

■ ■ ■

Mougins — 1975

Filet of Beef with
Raisin and Pepper Sauce

A glorified steak au poivre. The first time I tried it was with Vergé. It was sweet, spicy, beefy, and what I loved most was that it wasn't the classic creamy steak au poivre. It was more a sauce as you might serve with game. In fact you can apply this recipe to venison or bison.

For the Roasted Fingerling Potatoes:

1 tablespoon extra-virgin olive oil
1 pound fingerling potatoes, scrubbed and halved
     lengthwise
Salt and freshly ground white pepper
1 tablespoon unsalted butter
1 clove garlic, crushed
1 sprig thyme

Warm the oil in a large skillet over high heat. When the oil is hot, add the potatoes and season with salt and pepper. Brown evenly on all sides, turning as needed. Reduce the heat to medium, add the butter, garlic and thyme and cook until the potatoes are tender. Discard the garlic and thyme. Set the potatoes aside and keep warm.

For the Sautéed Spinach:

1 1/2 teaspoons unsalted butter
1 1/2 pounds spinach, stemmed and touch center
    veins removed
2 cloves garlic, crushed
Salt and freshly ground white pepper

Melt the butter in a large skillet over high heat. Add the spinach and garlic and season to taste with salt and pepper. Toss until the spinach is tender but still bright green, about 5 minutes. Discard the garlic and drain off any liquid remaining in the pan. Set aside and keep warm.

For the Beef and Sauce:

1/2 cup golden raisins
1/4 cup cognac or Armagnac
1 teaspoon coarsely crushed whole pink
    peppercorns
1 teaspoon coarsely crushed whole green
    peppercorns
1/2 teaspoon coarsely crushed whole black
    peppercorns
1/2 teaspoon coarsely crushed Szechuan peppercorns
1 whole Jamaican peppercorn, crushed
One 1 1/2 pound beef tenderloin, trimmed of fat and
    cut into 4 slices

Coarse salt
4 tablespoons unsalted butter
1/3 cup unsalted beef stock or low-sodium beef broth

1. Bring 2 cups of water to a boil in a small pot. Add the raisins, reduce the heat and simmer for 5 minutes. Drain and run the raisins under cold running water. Drain again. Put the raisins into a small bowl and pour the cognac over. Cover the bowl with plastic wrap and refrigerate overnight.

2. Combine the peppercorns together. Season the meat with the coarse salt and press the peppercorns into the beef. Warm 2 tablespoons butter in a large skillet over medium heat. Slip the filets into the pan and cook for 4 to 5 minutes on each side for medium-rare. Transfer the meat to a platter and keep warm.

3. Drain off the fat from the skillet. Add the raisins and cognac to the pan, return the pan to high heat and bring to a boil. Cook until the liquid is reduced by half. Add the beef stock, reduce the heat and simmer for 2 minutes. Cut the remaining 2 tablespoons butter into very small pieces. Gradually add the butter to the sauce, while continuously stirring. Season to taste for salt. Add the meat to the pan and baste with the sauce.

To serve: Divide the meat and sauce among four warm dinner plates. Serve with the fingerling potatoes and spinach.

Adapted from Roger Vergé's original recipe, as it appeared in *Roger Vergé's Cuisine of the South of France.* (William Morrow and Co., 1980).

■ ■ ■

Daniel Boulud

Copenhagen — 1977

Chestnut-Crusted Venison Loin

In Denmark, especially during hunting season, we served a lot of game. Elk and venison were particular favorites. In the restaurant we often served venison with huckleberry sauce. The chestnut crusted loin is an idea that came to me years later, but I think of it as an homage to my time in Denmark.

MAKES 6 SERVINGS

The crust:

³/₄ pound peeled fresh chestnuts
   (from about 1¹/₄ pounds in the shell), or
   ³/₄ pound dry-packed bottled or vacuum-sealed
   peeled fresh chestnuts

1. Break each chestnut into a few pieces and spread the pieces out on a baking sheet. Allow the pieces to dry overnight in a warm place—inside an oven with a pilot light is perfect.

2. The next day, place the chestnuts in the work bowl of a food processor and pulse until they break into ¹/₄-inch chunks. Sift the chestnuts, reserving the larger pieces that remain in the sieve, and discarding the pow-

der or saving it for another use. Transfer these pieces to a plate and keep close at hand.

The marinade:

1 teaspoon grated orange zest
$1/2$ cup freshly squeezed orange juice
2 tablespoons extra-virgin olive oil
1 teaspoon ground cinnamon
$1/2$ teaspoon freshly grated nutmeg
$1/4$ teaspoon ground star anise
$1/4$ teaspoon black peppercorns
2 cloves garlic, peeled and crushed
1 sprig thyme
Two $1^1/2$ pound venison loins, trimmed

Mix all the marinade ingredients together in a shallow pan, then roll the venison around in the marinade to coat. Cover the pan tightly with plastic wrap and refrigerate for at least 4 hours, or preferably overnight, turning the meat a few times during this period.

The rutabaga:

Zest from $1/2$ orange (pith removed), cut into very
   thin strands
2 tablespoons extra-virgin olive oil
1 large rutabaga, peeled, and cut into $1/2$-inch cubes
Large pinch of ground cinnamon

Small pinch of freshly grated nutmeg
Small pinch of ground star anise
1 clove garlic, peeled
1 sprig thyme
Salt and freshly ground pepper
1 cup unsalted chicken stock or low-sodium
   chicken broth

1. Put the orange zest in a small pot of water and bring to the boil. Boil 2 minutes; drain and set aside.

2. Warm the olive oil in a large sauté pan or skillet over medium heat. Add the rutabaga, spices, garlic, thyme, salt and pepper to taste and cook, stirring, for 5 minutes, without letting the rutabaga color. Add the chicken stock, bring to the boil, cover the pan and lower the heat to keep the liquid at a simmer. Braise the rutabaga for 15 minutes, or until it can be pierced easily with the tip of a knife.

3. Remove the cover and cook the rutabaga, stirring and turning it gently, until it is glazed and the liquid in the pan has evaporated; discard the garlic and thyme. Just before serving, stir in the orange zest. *(The rutabaga can be made several hours ahead, kept covered in the refrigerator, then warmed over gentle heat before serving; stir in the zest at serving time.)*

To cook the venison:

Salt and freshly ground white pepper
2 large eggs
1 large egg yolk
3 tablespoons all-purpose flour
$1/4$ cup extra-virgin olive oil

1. Center a rack in the oven and preheat the oven to 425°F.

2. Remove the venison from the marinade and discard the marinade. Pat the meat dry with paper towels and season with salt and pepper. In a pan or dish long enough to accommodate the venison loins, beat together the eggs and yolk. Dust one side of each loin with flour, shake off the excess and dip that side into the egg mixture and then into the chestnuts.

3. Heat the olive oil in a roasting pan over medium heat. When the oil is hot, add the venison, chestnut-side down, and cook for about 2 minutes. Turn the loins over and place the roasting pan in the oven. Roast the venison 10 to 12 minutes, until medium-rare. Pull the pan from the oven and transfer the loins to a warm platter. Set aside in a warm place while you make the sauce.

The sauce:

1 small shallot, peeled, trimmed, finely chopped,
   rinsed and dried
2 teaspoons coarsely crushed black pepper
1 teaspoon grated orange zest
4 teaspoons balsamic vinegar
1 cup dry red wine
1 teaspoon sugar
1½ cups unsalted beef stock or low-sodium beef broth
2 teaspoons unsalted butter

Remove as much grease from the liquid in the roasting pan as possible and place the pan over medium heat. Add the shallot and cook, stirring, just until translucent. Add the pepper and orange zest, sauté for a minute more, and then deglaze the pan with the balsamic vinegar, cooking and stirring until the vinegar just about evaporates. Add the red wine and cook down again until the pan is almost dry. Add the sugar and beef stock and cook at a boil until the liquid is reduced by half. Taste and add salt and pepper as needed. Remove the pan from the heat and swirl the butter into the sauce.

To serve: Slice the loins into 12 to 16 slices and arrange them attractively on a platter. Moisten with the sauce, and serve with the spiced rutabaga.

Originally appeared in the *Café Boulud Cookbook*.

■ ■ ■

Les Prés d'Eugénie — 1978

Caramelized Pears with Puff Pastry and Pear Cream

So simple in its ingredients yet requiring all the skills of the pastry chef: the flaky crust, the sweet poached fruit, the fluffy and deeply flavored cream. Here Guérard, the gastronomic chef, returns to the pastry kitchen where he started. Simple. Unforgettable.

MAKES 6 SERVINGS

For the Poached Pears:

1 moist, plump vanilla bean
3/4 cup sugar
Freshly squeezed juice of 1 lemon
3 ripe Bosc pears

Cut the vanilla bean lengthwise in half and, using the back of the knife, scrape the pulp out of the pod. Put the pulp and pod, sugar, and lemon juice in a medium pot with 1 quart water and bring to a boil. Lower the heat to keep the liquid at a simmer, peel the pears (you don't want to do this earlier—they'll darken), and add them to the pot. Cook the pears at a gentle simmer just until they can be pierced with the tip of a knife, 20 to 30 minutes. Remove the pot from the heat and allow the pears to cool in the poaching liquid. *(The pears can be made 3 days ahead and should be kept in their poaching syrup for storage in the refrigerator. Drain the fruit before using.)*

For the Pastry Cream:

1 moist, plump vanilla bean
2 cups whole milk
$^1/_2$ cup sugar
4 large egg yolks
3 tablespoons all-purpose flour
3 tablespoons cornstarch

1. Line a deep, rimmed plate with plastic wrap, leaving ample overhang. Cut the vanilla bean lengthwise in half and, using the back of the knife, scrape the pulp out of the pod.

2. Pour the milk into a medium saucepan. Stir in $^1/_4$ cup of the sugar, add the vanilla bean, pod and pulp, and bring to the boil. While the milk is coming to the boil, vigorously whisk the yolks and the remaining $^1/_4$ cup sugar together in a bowl until the mixture turns pale, then whisk in the flour and cornstarch.

3. Whisking without stop, very gradually add half the hot milk to the egg mixture. Pour into the saucepan and, still whisking constantly, cook over medium heat until the

pastry cream thickens and starts to boil. Allow the pastry cream to boil for 30 seconds, while constantly whisking, then scrape it onto the plastic-lined plate. Smooth the top of the cream with a rubber spatula and cover the cream with the overhanging plastic wrap (or another sheet of plastic). Press the plastic against the surface of the pastry cream—you don't want the cream to come in contact with air and develop a skin—and transfer the plate to the refrigerator until the cream is chilled. Remove the vanilla bean when the cream is cold. *(The pastry cream can be made up to 2 days in advance and kept covered airtight in the refrigerator. This recipe will make more cream than you need.)*

For the Puff Pastry:

1 sheet (about ½ pound) frozen puff pastry, thawed
1 egg, lightly beaten
Confectioners' sugar

1. Center a rack in the oven and preheat the oven to 425°F.

2. Cut the puff pastry into six 2- by 1½-inch rectangles and transfer to a baking sheet. Very gently brush with the beaten egg, being careful not to let wash run over the edges. Bake 10 to 12 minutes until golden brown. Remove the baking sheet from the oven. Preheat the broiler. Liberally dust the tops of the puff pastry with confectioner's sugar. Broil 30 seconds to 1 minute—

watch it closely—just until the sugar has melted and caramelized. Transfer the rectangles to a wire rack and let cool. Carefully split the top quarter of each rectangle from the bottom and set aside.

Assembly:

1 cup heavy cream
2 tablespoons pear brandy (Poire William)
Granulated sugar

1. Preheat the broiler.

2. Remove the pears from the poaching syrup with a slotted spoon. Carefully cut each pear in half lengthwise and core. Trim the pear halves so that they are the same size as the puff pastry rectangles and thinly slice them crosswise. Reserve the pear scraps. Transfer the pear halves to a lightly buttered baking sheet. Press on each pear half to fan slices toward the wider end. Sprinkle a liberal amount of sugar over the pears and broil 1 to 2 minutes—watch it closely—until the sugar is golden brown. (You can also caramelize the sugar with a blow torch or salamander.)

3. Coarsely chop the reserved pear scraps. Using a whisk, whip the heavy cream to medium peaks in a medium bowl. Whisk together $^1/_2$ cup pastry cream and the brandy in a separate mixing bowl. Gently fold the

whipped cream and the chopped pears into the pastry cream. Spoon about 2 tablespoons of the pear cream into the bottom of each puff pastry rectangle. Cover with the puff pastry top. Spread a thin layer of the pastry cream on top of the puff pastry. Using a spatula, place the caramelized pears on top. Serve immediately.

Adapted from Michel Guérard's original recipe, as it appeared in *Les Recettes Originales de Michel Guérard* (Éditions Robert Laffert, 1978).

■ ■ ■

Daniel Boulud

New York, Le Cirque — 1987

Bollito-Misto

The first thing I learned when I came to Le Cirque. A true "feast for the village." I can still envision the steam every time you opened the terrine and the inevitable "oohs and ahs" from the patrons. It takes a lot to get a Frenchman (especially a chef) to admit that another nation makes a better *pot-au-feu*, but on a *buon giorno*, it's hard to beat a bollito misto.

MAKES 12 TO 16 SERVINGS

For the Salsa Verde:

12 anchovies, finely chopped
6 tablespoons capers, rinsed, drained, and finely chopped
4 cloves garlic, finely chopped
1 bunch flat-leaf parsley, leaves only and finely chopped
$1/4$ bunch basil, leaves only and finely chopped
$3/4$ cup to 1 cup extra-virgin olive oil

Combine all the ingredients together. *(The sauce can be made 1 day in advance.)*

For Bollito Misto (should be made 1 day in advance):

2 pig's feet, each cut into 6 segments (ask your
    butcher to do this)
One 2-pound slab bacon
1 calf's head: de-boned, cut in half, rolled and tied
    (ask your butcher to do this)
1 veal shank, trimmed (ask your butcher to do this)
1 short rib
24 Yukon Gold potatoes, peeled
12 turnips, trimmed
12 large carrots, trimmed and cut in half
6 onions, peeled and studded with cloves
6 leeks, split lengthwise, washed and trimmed
2 bunches celery, trimmed and each stalk cut in half
2 bay leaves
1 tablespoon whole black peppercorns
1 fresh veal tongue
One 3-pound chicken, trussed
12 zampones or cotechinos, casing pricked
    with a fork

In the largest pot you have, add the pig's feet, bacon, calf's head, veal shank, short rib, potatoes, turnips, carrots, onions, leeks, celery, bay leaves and peppercorns. Add enough water to cover all the ingredients, about 4 to 5 gallons. Bring to a boil. Lower the heat and simmer, skimming the surface regularly, for 45 minutes.

Check the potatoes and if they are tender enough to be pierced with the point of a knife, remove them and transfer to a large bowl. Continue to cook for 1 hour and 15 minutes, while skimming the surface regularly. Transfer the remaining vegetables to a large bowl and set aside. Add the tongue and cook for 1 hour. Remove the pig's feets, bacon, and calf's head. Add the chicken and cook for 30 minutes. Add the sausage and cook for 30 minutes. Check to see if the chicken is tender and cooked through. Remove the meats from the broth. Strain the broth through a fine-mesh sieve and season to taste with salt and pepper, if needed. Refrigerate the meats and broth separately overnight. (The meats will be easier to slice when cold.)

To serve: Italian mustard fruits (mostarda di frutta), cut into 1/4-inch dice

Slice the meats. Rewarm the meats and the vegetables in the broth. Arrange the meats and vegetables on a large warm serving platter to be passed around. Place the broth in a soup tureen to be passed around. Serve with the salsa verde and Italian mustard fruits.

■ ■ ■

New York, DANIEL — 2000

Pancetta-Wrapped Tuna with Potato-Ramp Purée

A rustic yet majestic dish. I made this for Bill Clinton when he spent a weekend in East Hampton. I have yet to find someone who doesn't like this dish a lot, and I put in on the menu at least once a season. I suppose my favorite time, though, is in the spring when we get wild ramps from the Hudson Valley. In a way, this recipe is a summing up of where my career has taken me: the rare tuna is very *au courant* and New York-ish, and the pancetta is like the charcuterie I used to help my uncle make all those years ago.

MAKES 6 SERVINGS

The tuna:

8 to 10 ounces slab pancetta, thinly sliced, or an equal
   amount of sliced bacon
1¼ pounds tuna loin, cut like a roast,
   approximately 6 inches long, 1½ inches high,
   and 1½ inches wide
Salt and freshly ground pepper

Spread a piece of plastic wrap on the counter and lay out the slices of pancetta (or bacon) vertically, so that each slice overlaps its neighboring slice just a bit. Season the tuna very lightly with salt and pepper (remember, the pancetta or bacon is already salty) and place it cross-wise in the middle of the pancetta. One by one, wrap each piece of pancetta around the tuna, pressing the pancetta gently against the tuna and keeping the rows even. Secure the pancetta by tying the roast at 1 inch intervals with kitchen twine, just as you would a meat roast. Wrap the tuna in plastic wrap and refrigerate the tuna while you prepare the potatoes.

The potatoes and ramps:

$1^{3}/_{4}$ pounds potatoes, preferably fingerlings, peeled and cut into $^{1}/_{2}$ inch pieces
$^{3}/_{4}$ cup whole milk
8 tablespoons (1 stick) unsalted butter, cut into 8 pieces
3 ounces ramps, trimmed and washed or 3 ounces scallion greens (from about 4 to 5 ounces scallions) and 1 clove garlic, finely chopped
1 bunch Italian parsley, leaves only
4 tablespoons extra-virgin olive oil
Salt and freshly ground white pepper

1. Put the potatoes in a large pot of salted cold water, bring to the boil, and cook until the potatoes are tender enough to be pierced with the point of a knife, about 15 minutes.

2. While the potatoes are cooking, bring the milk and butter to the boil in a small saucepan. When the mixture reaches the boil and the butter melts, turn off the heat; keep this warm until you're ready to purée the potatoes.

3. When the potatoes are cooked through, drain them, then return them to the pot. Set the pot over medium heat and, shaking the pot to keep the potatoes from sticking, cook just until the potatoes are dry, a matter of a minute or two. Pull the pot from the heat and spoon the potatoes into a food mill fitted with the fine blade or a potato ricer. Push the potatoes through the food mill or ricer into a large bowl. In a slow, steady stream, add the hot milk and butter, stirring the liquid into the potatoes with a wooden spoon. Press a piece of plastic wrap against the surface of the potatoes and set the bowl aside in a warm place, or keep the potatoes warm in a covered heatproof bowl set over a pan of simmering water.

4. Bring a small pot of water to the boil. Toss the ramps or scallion greens into the pot and boil for 3 to 4 minutes, until tender. Scoop the ramps or scallions out of the pot with a slotted spoon (keep the boiling water over the heat) and run them under cold water to cool; dry them well. Toss the parsley into the boiling water and cook for 2 minutes before running it under cold water. When the parsley is cool, dry it as well.

5. Warm 1 tablespoon of the olive oil in a medium sauté pan or skillet over medium heat. If you're using it, add the garlic and sauté until it is tender but not colored, about 2 minutes. Toss in the ramps or scallions and cook, stirring, for 3 minutes. Scrape the ingredients into the container of a small processor or a blender. Add the drained and dried parsley and the remaining 3 tablespoons of olive oil and whir, scraping down the sides of the container as needed, until you have a smooth purée. Stir the purée into the potatoes, season with salt and pepper, cover again, and keep warm while you cook the tuna.

To finish:

3 tablespoons unsalted butter
6 ounces chanterelles, trimmed and cleaned (halved or quartered if large)
1 tablespoon finely chopped shallots, rinsed, and dried
Salt and freshly ground white pepper
1/4 cup sherry vinegar
1/4 cup dry white wine
1/4 cup homemade unsalted chicken stock, or store-bought low-sodium chicken broth
2 tablespoons finely chopped chives

1. Center a rack in the oven and preheat the oven to 350°F.

2. Warm 1 tablespoon of the butter in a large oven-proof sauté pan or skillet over medium heat and, when it's hot, slip the tuna into the pan. Sear the tuna for about 2 minutes on each of its four sides, then slide the pan into the oven for 5 minutes. (After 5 minutes in the oven, the tuna will be rare-cooked on the outside and warm but not colored anywhere else. If this is too rare for you, increase the tuna's time in the oven by 1 to 2 minutes, and you'll have medium tuna.) Lift the tuna out of the pan and onto a warm serving platter (don't discard the cooking fat).

3. Pour off half the cooking fat that's in the pan, return the pan to the stovetop, turn the heat to medium-low, and toss in the chanterelles. Cover the pan and cook the mushrooms until they're almost tender but not colored, 3 to 5 minutes. Add the shallots, season with salt and pepper, and cook another minute or so to soften the shallots. Pour in the vinegar and allow it to reduce by three quarters. Add the white wine, bring it to the boil, and allow it cook away before adding the chicken stock. Cook until the stock is reduced by half, then pull the pan from the heat and swirl in the remaining 2 tablespoons butter, a small piece at a time. (The idea is to melt the butter slowly so that it forms an emulsion.) Sprinkle in the chives.

To serve: Cut the tuna into 12 slices (this is done most easily with an electric knife or a very sharp, long, thin-bladed knife). On each of six warm dinner plates, center a scoop of potatoes, lean two slices of tuna against the potatoes, and surround with chanterelles and sauce.

Originally appeared in the *Café Boulud Cookbook*.

■ ■ ■

■ Acknowledgments

This project is different than any I had done before and would not have been possible without the assistance of countless friends and colleagues. I am grateful to them all:

First and foremost to Peter Kaminsky, for the countless hours he patiently recorded my ideas and guided my thoughts. His humor, style and in-depth knowledge of our industry allowed me to convey my views clearly and in a voice I could always call my own.

A special thanks to my Personal Assistant Hilary Tolman, who tirelessly oversaw so much of this project. Her meticulous organization is the driving force behind so much of what I do.

To Bob Tabian, my book agent, and the generous people at BASIC BOOKS: John Donatich, Liz Maguire, Megan Hustad, Jamie Brickhouse and Michelle Aielli.

To my inner-circle of kitchen family, Fabrizzio Salerni and Eric Bertoïa at DANIEL, Andrew Carmellini and George McKirdy, Zach Bell and Remy Fünfrock at

Café Boulud, Jean François Bruel and Cristina Aliberti at DB Bistro Moderne, for sharing with me your love of teaching and, of course, your love of cooking. And to Cyrille Allannic and Lior Lev Sercarz for testing the book's recipes. None of my books would ever be completed without my talented and indefatigable recipe editor, Katherine Yang.

As no kitchen staff could shine without the invaluable efforts of the front of the house, I thank Michael Lawrence, Marcus Draxler and Jean Luc Le Dû at DANIEL; Charles Pouchot, Dante Camara and Olivier Flosse at Café Boulud in New York; Philippe Langlois, Jonathon Dwight and Hanspeter Waechter at Café Boulud in Palm Beach; Jean Pierre François, Jerome Delpuch and Ryan Buttner at DB Bistro Moderne.

To my business partners, Joel Smilow and Lili Lynton, as well as my executive team of Brett Traussi, Guy Heksch, Georgette Farkas and Marcel Doron, for insisting we each give our very best everyday.

To all the Young Chefs who have worked in my kitchens, who have given their dedication, their energy, their willingness to learn. To the sous chefs, cooks, bakers, externs, stagiaires, and culinary students who have worked, 5 days or 5 years, as part of my *brigade*—I am thankful for your loyalty and commitment. It is so very rewarding to observe those of you who have passed through my doors and gone on to create and sustain your own extraordinary successes—in the US and around the world. There is no greater joy as a chef or mentor than knowing I have had some small influence on your careers. You make me proud and remind me why I am here in the first place.

To my entire restaurant staff—no chef operates in a vacuum. It takes teamwork from every member of the front and back of the house. You are all part of that which keeps my wheels turning and my dream possible. Every phone answered, every dish washed and every delivery inspected is vital.

To American cooking schools, who have transformed the landscape of culinary education over the last few decades. Their efforts have increased the respect and understanding of our profession in this country.

Of course to my mentors, Gerard Nandron, Georges Blanc, Roger Vergé, Michel Guérard and Sirio Maccioni for giving me the tools I needed and the lessons I learned. For allowing me to spread my wings and, when the time was right, fly on my own. And in memoriam, Jean Louis Palladin, for convincing me to come to New York and make my career and my home here.

To my wife Micky and my daughter Alix for their love, support and patience.

Finally, to my parents Julian and Marie Boulud as well as my Grandmère Francine, with whom my whole story begins and to whom I will always be grateful for their encouragement and support.

About the Author

Daniel Boulud was born in France in 1955 and raised on his family's farm near Lyon. He got his first restaurant job at the age of fourteen. After being nominated as a candidate for best cooking apprentice in France, Daniel went on to train under renowned chefs Roger Vergé, Georges Blanc and Michel Guérard. He then moved to the United States, where his first position was as Chef to the European Commission in Washington, D.C. From 1986 to 1992, he served as Executive Chef at New York's Le Cirque, regularly chosen as one of the highest rated in the country. In 1993, he opened Daniel, his signature restaurant and now Zagat's top-rated in New York City for two years running, followed by Café Boulud in 1998 and db bistro Moderne in 2001. Among numerous other awards, he has been named "Chef of the Year" by *Bon Appétit*, and his restaurant, Daniel, received *Gourmet*'s "Top Table" award. On March 14, 2001, the *New York Times* awarded the restaurant the coveted four stars.